THE GIDEONS

THE GIDEONS

The story of The Gideons
International in the
British Isles

PHYLLIS THOMPSON

HODDER AND STOUGHTON
LONDON SYDNEY AUCKLAND TORONTO

British Library Cataloguing in Publication Data

Thompson, Phyllis, *1926–*
  The Gideons.——(Hodder Christian paperbacks)
  1. Gideons International——History
  I. Title
  220′.06′041   BV2370.G5

ISBN 0 340 34248 X

Hodder and Stoughton Editorial Office: 47 Bedford Square, London WC1B 3DP

To Norman, my brother

Acknowledgments

My thanks and gratitude go to a number of Gideons and members of The Auxiliary for providing material for this book, especially Mr. C.A. Clark, Mr. R. Norman Wyatt, Mr. Henry M. Sibthorpe, Mr. Arthur Rousham, Mrs. E.F. Dalgleish; also to the Rev. Montague H. Knott for invaluable information about the beginning of the work in the British Isles; to the Rev. Ian Coffey and the Rev. Vic Jackopson for sharing their experiences; to Miss Katie Hunt for typing the manuscript; and above all to Mr. and Mrs. Ian Hall, whose unfailing help and encouragement from beginning to end have made the task such a pleasant one.

Contents

1   Introducing The Gideons

When Ian Hall agreed to stand in for his friend and arrange a dinner for business executives in one of the best hotels in Bangalore, he did not really know what he was letting himself in for. Bill Nelson had just told him, "I've promised to arrange meetings for a fellow from England who wants to start The Gideons here in South India. I've made a few arrangements, but now I've had this urgent call from Pakistan, so I can't finish the job. Can you help me out? Meet him at the airport, book him in at the hotel for a few days, keep an eye on him? You will? Thanks a lot, Ian. So grateful to you . . ."

Ian had no idea who or what The Gideons were, and was quite surprised when one of the Indian business men to whom he mentioned the matter observed casually, "The Gideons? They're the Bible people, aren't they? Put Bibles in hotels." He evidently knew a lot more than Ian knew. Further enquiry elicited the information that he had seen Bibles with a Gideon emblem in hotel bedrooms when travelling in the USA. All the hotels there seemed to have them, he said, and he evinced a measure of interest in the forthcoming visit.

"Coming to Bangalore to tell us about themselves? Yes, if I'm free I'd like to hear what they've got to say. Quite interesting." So he had little difficulty in fixing up the dinner party, and as Bill had told him there would be nothing for him to do – the fellow coming out from England would do all the talking – he decided he'd sit back and enjoy it all. It wasn't every day he had the opportunity to eat in a four-star hotel, relax in an air-conditioned room afterwards, and just listen to someone else holding forth. It would make a nice change, he told Rita. Pity it was for men but not their wives, or she could have come along too.

And now the time had come. He'd met the visitor at the airport, spotting him immediately as he emerged from the plane – an elderly man, sturdily built, wearing a panama hat, the only European, looking like a pigeon among the starlings in that stream of dark-skinned Indians crossing the tarmac.

"Mr. Bradbury? Welcome to Bangalore!" he'd said, and whisked him off to his hotel, to return a few hours later in time to give him a little information about the invited guests. Briefly he went through the list, making a few comments.

K.C. Abraham, managing director of Bolsts, the exporters... Mr. Koshy, owner of a big restaurant and a general store... Iain Phillips, an electrical engineer, an Anglo Indian... George Benjamin, an executive with the Hindustan Aircraft Corporation... and so on. "They all speak English, of course. No need for me to interpret for you. Ah, they've started coming. Glad to see you! This is Mr. Frederick W. Bradbury from London . . ."

They were all in western dress except the deputy chief engineer of Southern Railways, who turned up in his national dress, grinning cheerfully at Ian and quick with reminiscences of fifteen years before, when the two of them were young officers together in the Indian Army. Conversation was easy at the dinner table, for most of the men knew each other, and if from time to time they lapsed into Malayālam, they soon reverted to English out of respect for their host, formerly the national secretary of The Gideons in England. It was he they had come to meet, more especially to hear, and Ian, who had noticed his rather diffident manner, as though somewhat bewildered by his surroundings, wondered uneasily if he would be able to grip their attention.

He need not have worried. Within a few minutes, once they were up in his private room and settled back in their wicker chairs, their eyes were riveted on the animated face of the man who had risen promptly to his feet to address them. There was nothing diffident about him now. He stood there, Bible in hand, and his theme soon became apparent – how God was using this Book through The Gideons.

The Gideons – who were they? Just ordinary business men like themselves, he told them, men who believed the Bible was the Word of God and who knew from personal experience that it was *alive*! They weren't preachers or pastors or evangelists or missionaries by vocation – they were in the workaday world to buy and sell, to provide facilities that people would pay for, and they travelled about to do it. They were men who knew what it was like to arrive in a hotel in a strange city, alone.

... Alone in a hotel bedroom, far from home – that's where John found himself that night when, drunk as usual, he couldn't get to sleep. Home was away in Texas, and the only news his father got of him was when bills or cheques that had bounced arrived from indignant creditors, demanding payment for his son's debts. Not that it worried John. It was not the thought of his misdemeanours that was keeping him awake, it was just that his pillow was so uncomfortable.

"Feels as though there's a brick underneath," he thought irritably, and pulling the pillow away, to his surprise he found not a brick, but a Bible. Whoever had made up the bed after the last guest must have missed it. His interest was aroused sufficiently for him to look at the introductory notes and turn up some of the verses, but he was too bemused to read them. Not until the early hours of the morning was he sober enough to do so. Rolling over on the bed, he looked at the Bible he had left open, picked it up and started to read.

Then something he hadn't expected happened. His eyes fell on the words: "He that believeth on the Son hath everlasting life; and he that believeth not the Son shall not see life; but the wrath of God abideth on him."

That verse seemed to be directed straight at him, like an accusing finger, and he was suddenly aware that he was not alone. God was there, a silent Presence waiting for him to face reality, to decide what he would do in the light of those words in the Bible before him.

How long he remained there, wrestling with himself, he did not know, but in the end he came to his decision. He went to the telephone directory, looked up the number of a Baptist minister, and put through a call. He was in real trouble, he said, and wanted help. He wanted to become a Christian.

The Gideons' representative from London paused at that point, mopped his head, and proceeded, impressively.

"He became a Christian. His wife had left him, but she took him back, and she, too, became a Christian.

"I know him well. He is now a Gideon and actively involved in the overseas outreach through the International Extension Committee. He has a special reason for being interested in The Gideons. You see, the Bible he'd found under his pillow had been left in the room by them."

No one stirred. From the distance came the muted sound of traffic, nearer at hand the incessant grinding of the cicadas but inside there was silence. Ian glanced at the men sitting around the softly lighted room, saw the expressions of awakening excitement on their faces, was conscious of it himself, and gave himself up to listen. The speaker had plenty to say.

Another Bible that had been placed in a hotel by The Gideons saved a man from suicide. It was in one of the south-western states of the USA, where a lot of hard-drinking men were working for a government construction company. Their paymaster, Big John, was an inveterate gambler, and one week he had a run of bad luck. He gambled away his own money, then borrowed the wages of the whole company – and lost the lot. That was when he decided the only way out was to end his life, and that is what he was planning to do when his eyes fell on the Bible in his hotel room. He picked it up, and it fell open at Isaiah: "Seek the Lord while he may be found." It brought him up with a start. "Seek the Lord... let the wicked forsake his way ... let him return to the Lord, that he may have mercy upon him ..."

"Seek the Lord..." Big John did just that. The night hours saw him on his knees in the silence of his room, and very early the next morning he did the best thing he could have done. He went to see the manager. He wanted to confess the whole thing, come what may, and he told his story from beginning to end, right up to the reading of those verses in the Bible, his decision to forsake the wrong way and return to the Lord. And at that point the mercy began to work.

The manager, who had listened in quiet amazement as Big John told of his experience during the night, sat silent for a few moments, then reached out his hand for the phone. He wanted to speak to the owner of the casino where Big John had been gambling. "Tony, can you come over? It's important. There's something you ought to know." Tony came over, and Big John again told his story. Tony, like the manager, was impressed by Big John's humble confession, both of his crime and his reaction to what he had read in the Bible. He was also alerted to the possibility of his casino becoming uncomfortably involved in a government payroll scandal.

"Look here," he said. "I'll pay you all the money back on one condition – that you never come gambling in my casino again."

The condition presented no problem to Big John. He was through with gambling. The sequel to the story was not only that his life was changed and that he became an earnest Christian and a lay reader, but that Tony was also converted – and *he* became a Gideon.

Then there was the case of the woman who was so hostile to Christianity that, finding a Gideon Bible in her hotel bedroom, she threw it irritably on top of a cupboard out of her sight. But somehow, it was not out of her mind. She felt as though it were shooting flashes of lightning at her head as she sat writing letters, and rising angrily she leapt on her chair, snatched the Bible down, put it outside the door into the corridor, and locked herself into her room.

Even that did not work. She could not rest, and in the end she opened the door, picked up the Bible, and started to read.

"And so that woman in Sweden read through the night, and came to salvation . . ."

"In Sweden?" one of the Indians said in astonishment.

Oh yes, there were Gideons in Sweden too, and in Australia, and Mexico and Hong Kong – in fact, there were Gideons in about fifty different countries. It was a sort of international club, uniting Christian business men irrespective of race or colour. It was the badge that did it. The Gideons' representative from Great Britain glowed with enthusiasm. One of the thrills of his first year as a Gideon had been to go into a restaurant in London one day and see two men wearing The Gideons' badge – they were from Japan, on their first visit to England. Brothers in Christ, needing no introduction!

The badge. It was amazing how well known it had become. Prince Philip, the Duke of Edinburgh, spotted a man wearing it at some function, went and spoke to him, told of how he'd found a Gideon Bible in a hotel where he was staying, read some of the verses indicated. Found them very helpful, too, he said. One never knew who would read the Bibles that The Gideons had placed in hotel bedrooms.

Not that they put them there personally, of course, the speaker explained. Some people got the mistaken idea that Gideons went snooping along hotel corridors slipping Bibles into bedrooms when no one was looking. Not at all! That wasn't the Gideon method. Gideons were known and respected members of their own communities, and it was as such that they approached the hotel managers with their offer of free Bibles for every bedroom. At the same time they explained what The Gideons stood for. It was a very simple, straightforward way of using their status in society to disseminate the Word of God and witness to their faith. Then, if the manager accepted the offer, they fixed a date to take along the Bibles and hold a little dedication ceremony, complete with display, in the hotel lounge.

When, in Great Britain, The Gideons had distributed one million copies of the Word of God, they held a special ceremony in a West End hotel to mark the occasion, presenting the proprietor with an embossed commemorative Gideon Bible. That was away back in 1957. They would soon be reaching the two-million mark, and would be arranging for a presentation in the Hilton in Park Lane.

The attention of those Indian men in the world of trade was gripped. A presentation in the Hilton! This was salesmanship, the sort of enterprise their firms employed to advertise their goods. They exchanged surprised glances and leaned forward to listen as the speaker went on:

"We're ordinary business men, and we employ business methods, because we are in business – in business for God. We do His work the best way we know. It's His money we're investing, and we look for returns.

"What returns? Not returns in cash, but returns in souls, Souls of men and women and boys and girls who have been reached by the Spirit of God as they have looked into those Bibles. I wish you could come into The Gideons' office and open the mail with me. What a thrill, day after day, to receive letters from people who have come across a Gideon Bible, seen our address in it, and written in because they want to know more!" And he went on to tell of the joy of replying to those letters, counselling by post people he would never have met in the ordinary course of his life. A letter from a prisoner in Liverpool jail, for instance:

Dear Secretary,

Would you please put me in touch with someone who is interested in the likes of myself (a convicted prisoner). I am afraid, sir, though yet still only 28 years of age, I have been in prison a number of times; in fact, the past seven years have been mostly spent in prison, my last sentence being five years, this one three years.

In these years I have lost my people, first my father, then, when once more I turned off that right road, I lost my mother. I feel sure in my heart, they both died of a broken heart, for my way of life. I was till now so in the dark. I am truly sorry I am seeing the light of life a while too late, for them, too, to see I had found what I'd lost . . .

I do not for one moment think I can do all the Bible tells us to do or not to do, but I shall try to live as near to its ways as I possibly can. Then one day I may be told, "Your sins are forgiven you".

If anyone would care for a visit order to come to see me, please write . . .

The great advantage of The Gideons organisation was that there was someone on the spot to follow up the opening. The local Gideons ensured that that young man was told he did not have to wait until he had fulfilled all the law to have his sins forgiven, the national secretary from England was explaining when he was interrupted again.

"Do The Gideons distribute Bibles in prisons?" asked one of the men, leaning forward with a perplexed expression. "I thought they only provided them for hotels."

"Oh yes, The Gideons distribute Bibles in prisons, and in schools and hospitals as well. Let me tell you about the thirteen-year-old schoolboy who, along with others, was given a New Testament on moving to another school. He took it home, showed it to his father, and his father was so angry he warned him that if he ever found him reading it, he'd get a good thrashing. Well, the boy went on reading it, and the father went on thrashing him until, in the end, he took the Testament and tore it up and threw it out.

"But just at that point the Holy Spirit began to work in his heart. What was it about that little book that was so fascinating that this son of his would be willing to take two severe beatings just for the joy of reading it? So off he went into the yard, collected the scattered pages when no one was looking, put it together, and began to read . . . He is now converted, and so is the whole family!

"Then there is the case of the girl who had refused to

read the Bible for years, to the sorrow of her mother, but when she was ill in hospital there was a Gideon Testament by her bed, and she started reading . . .''

He was off again, with story after story of the effect of Gideon Bible distribution in the traffic lanes of life, the places where people were in transit, away from familiar surroundings, bewildered and often lonely. What opportunities he had had sitting in his office answering telephone calls, entertaining unexpected visitors, from men just out of prison to guests from first-class hotels, replying to letters from earnest-minded schoolchildren, to people dying in hospital, all of them getting in touch because of those copies of the Word of God that had been placed by The Gideons!

''Where we know the need we will sow the seed!'' His talk was peppered with pithy sayings, the eloquent salesman's stock in trade, and his listeners' eyes twinkled as he came out with them. There was also an organisation for the wives of Gideons, he told them. It was called The Auxiliary and it was they who made the presentations of New Testaments to trainee nurses. However, their main task was to support their husbands in every way possible, especially by prayer.

''The Auxiliaries on their knees keep The Gideons on their toes!'' he said with a triumphant grin. An important aspect of The Gideons' organisation was the involvement of their wives.

He was giving them an all-over picture of the work he had come to represent, and as he stood there, mopping his face from time to time, his own enthusiasm for it was its best advertisement.

''He's really sold on his job,'' thought Ian Hall rather wistfully. He himself spent much of his time in an office, as business manager of a large mission high school, but he rarely received such letters, visitors and telephone calls as this short-necked, beetle-browed, elderly visitor from London was describing.

''And how did all this start?'' he was saying now. ''This organisation of Christian business men that is reaching

people who might otherwise never read the Word of God –
how did it all begin?

"I'll tell you," he went on. "It started when a twelve-
year-old American boy named John Nicholson promised
his dying mother that he would read a portion of the Bible
every day. Thirty years later he was still keeping his
promise when, as an ordinary salesman travelling in
paper, he went late one evening to book a room in a hotel
in Wisconsin, USA . . ." and he went on to outline briefly
the sixty-year-old history of The Gideons, not forgetting
the story of the wealthy businessman whose visit to
Honolulu resulted in the distribution of New Testaments
to the entire Pacific Fleet of the US Navy based at Pearl
Harbor, some months before the historic bombing by the
Japanese brought America into the Second World War.
"And on the bodies of some of those American sailors
washed up on the beaches were found Gideon New
Testaments, with the names of their owners written under
a declaration of their faith in Jesus Christ. . .

"And this is the organisation that has come to India.
You all know of Heinz products – 57 different varieties!
Well, Leonard Crimp, vice-president of Heinz, is a
Gideon, and he came to North India a year or two ago and
established branches there – in Delhi, Bombay, Madras. . .

"Now is the time to get started down here in Bangalore.
If just six of you enrol as members, a branch can be
started."

But more than six enrolled that night, as hands were
stretched out eagerly and dark eyes scanned the application forms to ensure that all requirements could be met.

Any professional or businessman, except those engaged
in the manufacture or sale of alcoholic drinks, is eligible
for membership. No person shall be admitted to
membership unless he be a professional or businessman
who believes in the Bible as the inspired Word of God,
believes in the Lord Jesus Christ as the Eternal Son of
God, has received Him as his personal Saviour,
endeavours to follow Him in his daily life, and is a

member of good repute in a Christian Church,
Congregation or Assembly.

Ian Hall wanted to join too. He saw in this organisation a
means of penetrating into strata of society not easily
reached by normal methods. "May I have an application
form, please?" he asked. "I'd like to become a Gideon."

He was quite unprepared for the reaction of the
representative from Great Britain. "I'm afraid you're not
eligible, Mr. Hall," he said rather apologetically. Ian was
taken aback, and stared at him in surprise. "But Mr.
Bradbury – why ever not?"

"Well, you're a missionary, aren't you?"

"Yes."

"That's what puts you out. The Gideons are not for
ministers or preachers or evangelists or missionaries. It's a
layman's organisation, for men engaged in business. I'm
sorry, Mr. Hall."

"Oh, that's all right. I quite understand," replied Ian
easily. All the same, he felt a twinge of envy as he saw those
Indians he knew so well grouping together, arranging for
their first meeting, heard them planning how they'd make
a start at Bible distribution, what address they'd use on
their literature.

"It's all a much bigger affair than I thought it was," he
told his wife later. "Amazing opportunities, right out of
our world! And to think it all started with one American
commercial traveller, going his rounds!" Then he added,
rather slowly: "You know, Rita, for the first time in my
life, I wish I wasn't a missionary."

2   How it All Started

When John Nicholson pushed through the swing doors of
the Central House Hotel in Boscobel, Wisconsin that
September evening in 1898, all he wanted was to get to bed
as soon as possible. It had been a busy day and he was tired,
lugging his case of samples around to the various firms
who might give him an order for paper, grinning
cheerfully at the managers who snorted that they had no
time to waste on commercial travellers, listening patiently
to those who all too evidently had. Life on the road was
like that, you had to take the gruff with the garrulous if
you wanted to do business. Now that part of it was over for
another day, and there was still a lot that he had to do
before he could stretch out and get to sleep. He went up to
the reception desk, dumped his bags down, smiled at the
clerk who knew him well and said,

"A room for the night, please." Then his face dropped
as the clerk shook his head regretfully and replied,

"Sorry, Nick. The place is full. Haven't got a room left."

"Oh, say!..." – it was 9 o'clock already, and the
prospect of going off to find accommodation somewhere
else was a gloomy one – "I always come here." He looked
around for the landlord. "Can't you find a corner for me
somehow?"

The landlord was in a dilemma. Nicholson was a good
customer, and one who gave no trouble. He looked around
the lobby where one drunk was already stretched out in a
corner, where a couple of poker games were in progress
that he knew might end in a fight, heard the loud voices
that were coming through the open door of the bar-room,
and sighed. He did not like to turn away the respectable
sort of person whose presence gave his hotel a good name,
but what was he to do?

Then his eye lighted on a small, quietly-dressed man in his early thirties who was sitting at a table writing, and he exclaimed,

"Wait a minute, Nick! See that fellow over there writing up his orders? He's on the road, like you. Travelling in paint for Hookers of Chicago. Seems a decent sort of chap. Name of Hill. There's a spare bed in his room, and if you're both willing to share, you could have it."

"Let's go right across and ask him," responded Nicholson promptly. And so it came about that he and Samuel Hill were brought together. Neither had the least presentiment of what that apparently chance meeting was to lead to. They just nodded in a friendly way to each other, Nicholson noted the number of their room and said,

"You finish writing up your orders, Mr. Hill. I'll go on up to our room and write mine there." The place was thick with tobacco smoke, and he would be glad to get out of it. "Come on up when you're ready. You won't disturb me," and off he went.

There was no table in the sparsely furnished bedroom, but he moved the basin and water jug off the marble-topped wash-stand and settled down to the journeyman's last task of the day. He was hard at work when his room-mate arrived, and Hill undressed quietly, slipped into his bed, and was soon asleep. Nicholson wrote on till at last he had dealt with his final order, then he quietly gathered the papers together and tucked them into his bag, and with a sigh of relief stretched out his hand for the book he had carefully laid aside, and moved the lamp nearer to him. This was the best part of the day for him. He could relax, direct his thoughts into another channel. But just then there was a movement from the other bed. Hill rolled over, opened his eyes, and looked around.

"Say, I'm sorry about this," said Nicholson contritely, thinking he had awakened him. "Please excuse me if I keep this light on a little while longer." Then he continued in explanation, "I always make it a practice to read the Word of God," and he held up the book that was in his hand, "and speak to Him before I retire."

He was quite unprepared for the effect of his words on his companion. A sneer, a polite murmur, an indifferent shrug would not have surprised him, nor abashed him either. He was accustomed to them all, and being what is known as a thorough-going extrovert, was undaunted by any of them. But the man in the bed reacted in none of these ways. Instead, as though galvanised into life, he sat bolt upright, his face aglow, and said,

"Read it aloud. Let me join you. I'm a Christian, too."

So Nicholson read the fifteenth chapter of the Gospel according to John, and they knelt and prayed together. They found that they had so much in common that they talked until two o'clock in the morning.

"Like a couple of schoolgirls," laughed Nicholson. It was exciting and heart-warming to meet a fellow-believer so unexpectedly – better than a tonic! And how nearly they had missed it! Among the many things he said that night was that it would be a good idea to form a Christian association for commercial travellers. It could transform life for them to meet other like-minded fellows at the end of the day – an oasis in the midst of the smoke and drink of the bar.

Hill agreed warmly. They must do it – but how would they know each other?

A badge. They'd need a badge.

That was it. A Christian association for commercial travellers, and a badge to recognise each other. This really was the right idea. They must get it going, they agreed. Finally they fell asleep.

That was as far as it got. The next morning there were samples to be sorted, hurried breakfasts to be eaten, bills to be paid, trains to catch. There was no time to talk, and the two men went their separate ways without arranging anything. The idea lay dormant.

Their paths did not cross for eight months, and when eventually they did, it was entirely due to an unforeseen rearrangement of Nicholson's programme which delayed him for a day, bringing him early in the morning face to face in the street with Hill, who was on his way to the station.

It was a moment of destiny. The essence of eternity was in it. So life's opportunities come, unheralded and unobserved. The two men, hurrying in opposite directions, recognised each other immediately, and their faces lit up with pleasure at the meeting. And what sprang to the minds of both of them was the idea of an association that they had discussed, but about which they had done nothing. Within the few minutes they stood talking together they agreed to call a meeting to form an association for Christian commercial travellers on July 1st, 1899, at 2 p.m. in the YMCA there in Janesville. That would give them two months in which to publicise it. Then Hill hurried off to catch his train and Nicholson to his round of calls. It must be "business as usual" for both of them, but with an additional reason for being on the alert. Who among their business acquaintance would be likely to help launch this new association?

No record remains of the number of men they spoke to about the projected inaugural meeting, or how many they hoped would attend. In the event, only one turned up. William Knights, who travelled in the grocery line and lived in Janesville, had responded to the idea with enthusiasm as soon as Nicholson told him of it, and had written round to all the people he could think of who might be interested. He arrived punctually on the day appointed, and so, of course, did the other two, but they waited in vain for anyone else to join them. So there they were, the three of them, and they had to decide what to do now – to call the whole thing off in the face of such an evident lack of interest, or to go ahead and form the association in spite of it.

They decided to go ahead. They bowed their heads in prayer. The next step was to elect officers. Sam Hill was proposed and seconded as chairman, Will Knights as vice-chairman and John Nicholson as secretary and treasurer. Nick was the one who had the idea in the first place, the others said, so he was the one to do the work. He grinned down at them from his six-foot height, accepted the challenge, and then they got down to business.

Membership. Who could be accepted as members? They

were agreed on the qualifications necessary. The members must be commercial travellers, and they must be those who openly acknowledged their faith in Christ, and who believed that the Bible was true – all of it. So that was settled, too.

Then came up the question of a name. What should they call themselves? The name was important, but no suggestion either of them made met with the approval of the other two. "Christian Commercial Travellers of America" was accurate enough, but too much of a mouthful, but they could think of nothing else. In the end one of them said slowly,

"If God is in this thing, He will give us a name." The other two nodded rather solemnly. "If God is in this thing." By this time they were pretty sure that He was.

"Let's pray about it." So they prayed, lapsing eventually into silence as they waited. Then Will Knights raised his head and said clearly,

"I believe I've got it. We'll be The Gideons," and bringing out his Bible he read aloud, from the Book of Judges, the familiar record of Gideon and his 300 men who silently surrounded the camp of the enemy, each carrying a pitcher with a lighted flare inside it, and at a given signal suddenly broke their pitchers, held their flares aloft and shouted, "The sword of the Lord and of Gideon!"

When Knights came to the words, "They stood every man in his place round about the camp," he paused significantly. It was not necessary to labour the point. The other two men saw it quickly. Those 300 men held their torches up just where they were standing, and spoke up just where they were.

The Gideons. This was it! They would be modern Gideons, standing in their place and speaking up for what they believed as they went about their territory on their job.

The association was founded, the officers elected, the name chosen. Samuel E. Hill, travelling in paint for Hookers, John H. Nicholson, travelling in paper for

Bradner's, and William J. Knights travelling in groceries for Gould's, went home.

The pump had been primed, and now the flow started. Within a month another nine men had been recruited, and The Gideons held their first business meeting. The matter of a badge came up. They needed a badge so that they could recognise each other, but what was it to be? Any ideas? One of the members indicated that he had one. He proposed that the emblem should suggest the weapons Gideon's 300 men used in that historic battle, and went on to draw rapidly the design of a circle with a white pitcher on a blue background, and a little red flame coming out of the top of the pitcher. The circle, he explained, was for the trumpet which each man sounded, thus completing the analogy.

The emblem was adopted without delay, and now things went with a swing. Exactly one year after the meeting when three men founded The Gideons, 600 members had been enrolled, thirty-seven of whom managed to attend the two-day conference that was held for mutual encouragement and discussion as to how the association could be furthered.

"One year ago we looked forward, little knowing what the year would bring forth," said Sam Hill in his presidential address. "Today we look backward to see a year filled with blessings, enriched with fulfilled promises and realised hope . . . Who dare predict what the future has in store for us? But however large and powerful the Gideon army may become I shall always thank God that He permitted me to have some part in its beginning." Then he added a little quotation from the prophecy of Zechariah: "Who hath despised the day of small things?"

The day of small things had passed already, that soon became evident. John Nicholson, as secretary, was swamped with correspondence and the keeping of accounts. In a couple of years it had become more than he could cope with, and in 1905 a full-time, salaried secretary was appointed, and an office opened in Chicago.

It was in that same year that a Gideon from Chicago had

occasion to travel to the British Isles in the course of his
business. While there he discovered that a Christian
Association for Commercial Travellers had been in
existence for some thirty years, and he set out to discover
more about it.

One aspect of its activities particularly impressed him.
In order to make things more congenial for travellers who
were so often away from home, the Association was
placing a few books for wholesome reading in the hotels
they frequented, and in these miniature libraries there was
always a copy of the Bible. This was a splendid idea, the
Chicago Gideon decided, and made a special note of it in
the report that he made on his return to the USA.

"They do not hold their meetings in churches, as we do.
They hold their meetings among themselves, and do
personal work on the road amongst their fellow travellers."
Then he added words which were to point the way to what
later proved The Gideons' most distinctive activity, that
for which they were to become known throughout the
western world.

"They are doing a great work by putting Bibles in all the
rooms of the different hotels they go to. This is a grand
work, and I think we ought to adopt the same."

If the organisation had continued to move forward
smoothly no doubt the Chicago Gideon's suggestion
would have been put into action without delay. But
instead, it ran into financial difficulties from which it only
emerged after three or four years. It was not until 1908 that,
at their annual convention, The Gideons pledged
themselves to the task of getting Bibles placed in every
hotel in the country.

It was an ambitious aim, and a challenging one. They
had no very clear idea as to how they were to achieve it, but
what they lacked in foresight they made up for in
enthusiasm, and the collection bags fairly overflowed with
donations for the new project.

The idea caught fire. The Gideon general secretary was
full of it and when, a short time later, he was given ten
minutes in which to speak at a ministers' fraternal in

Cedar Rapids, Iowa, he could talk of nothing else. By the time he sat down the friendly, impersonal interest of the ministers in an association for Christian commercial travellers had quickened into a lively desire to have a share in what they were planning to do. When the pastor of the First Presbyterian Church rose to his feet and proposed that Gideon Bibles be placed in all the local hotels, and that the local churches, not The Gideons, should foot the bill, the motion was carried unanimously. Financially the project got off the ground with surprising rapidity.

The Gideons, however, soon found themselves encountering difficulties of another nature. Their idea was not merely to get Bibles placed in hotels without any sort of introduction or explanation. If a visitor in a hotel picked up a Bible, he might have no idea where to start reading, and they proposed inserting a page inside the front cover making some suggestions, as well as giving the address of their headquarters for the sake of anyone who might want to write for further help.

The obvious thing to do was to place an order for several thousand Bibles, complete with the Gideon insertion, with the American Bible Society. This, however, proved impossible. Under their charter, the Society is under an obligation to issue the Bible "entirely without note or comment." When 6,000 Bibles were delivered at the YMCA in Chicago, therefore, the local Gideons had the job of pasting in the insertions themselves. Fortunately for them, the role of a Gideon's wife had early been categorically defined as an Auxiliary, so Auxiliaries could be called upon to help in that sort of emergency. But with the increasing demand for Bibles it eventually became necessary to become their own publishers – a mammoth task, especially when it came to proof-reading.

Meanwhile, the Bible distribution had started, almost before they were ready for it. They had planned to start approaching hotel managers, offering to supply them with Bibles free of charge. To their surprise the scheme suddenly went into reverse when a hotel manager in Iron Mountain, Montana, approached them with a request for twenty-five Bibles, and enclosed a cheque to cover the cost. Less than a month later another order for Bibles came, this time from Detroit, Michigan – "151 Bibles, please, remittance enclosed." So the Bible distribution got under way, and the results far exceeded expectations. The headquarters in Chicago started to hum with excitement as letters came pouring in from people who had reached a crisis in their lives through what they had read in the Bible so surprisingly found in their hotel bedrooms. And Gideons in various places found themselves receiving urgent messages from headquarters asking them to go and visit someone living in their neighbourhood who had written in because he wanted to get in touch with God, and didn't know how. Things were moving fast.

Meanwhile, the advantages to men who travelled on business of belonging to a sort of Christian club, with its opportunities of fraternising with like-minded people, was attracting attention. Why must The Gideons be confined to those who came into the rather limiting category of "commercial travellers"? Why could not men in executive positions join, and even professional men whose careers involved a lot of travelling? It could be very lonely, going far distances and putting up in strange hotels where one didn't know a soul. The wearing of a Gideon badge, and introductions to fellow Gideons on the way, could transform things for them, too, and their need for the right sort of companionship was just as great, if not greater, than those who moved around in a more limited territory. These arguments won the day, and gradually the basis of membership was broadened to include all business and professional men who were constantly "on the road", and who adhered to the evangelical Christian faith – and were prepared to say so.

Being prepared to say so was a qualification for Gideon membership. A Gideon was not expected to keep quiet about what he believed. Timid souls soon backed out as unobtrusively as they had slipped in, returning to the comfortable anonymity of those who explain that their faith is a private affair, and who do nothing further about it. In spite of these withdrawals the organisation continued to grow, and by 1947 it was known nation-wide.

Then things began to take a new turn. The Second World War was over at last, the battered nations, the defeated and the victorious alike, were catching their breath and licking their wounds – but, for all that, a spirit of enterprise was in the air. The Gideons in America decided that the time had come to look beyond their own borders.

Over the years some sporadic efforts had been made to introduce the Gideon association elsewhere. In fact, as far back as 1903, a Glasgow business man travelling in the USA happened to attend a meeting at which Nicholson and Hill were speaking, and at the end enthusiastically joined their ranks. Robert McInnes thereby went down in the annals of history as being the first Gideon member outside the territorial limits of the USA. But although, at various times, Bibles had been placed in such widely different countries as Japan and Java, Bermuda and Burma, Sweden and Syria, very little had been accomplished in the way of establishing Gideon centres outside the USA apart from Canada.

This state of things must not be allowed to continue. In the autumn of 1947 The Gideons International Extension Committee was formed. Its aim was not to place Bibles in hotels in other countries. Its aim was to establish Gideon centres in other countries. The placing of Bibles would inevitably follow. And if there was one country more than another in which the Committee wanted to see that happen, it was Great Britain. Allies during two world wars, speaking a common language and sharing to a great degree a common heritage, what more natural than that the business men of these two countries should be further linked by this association for those of a common faith?

On the face of it, it should have been easy. It turned out to be uncommonly difficult.

3 First British Gideons

The British, it must be admitted, are not the easiest people in the world with whom to work. For one thing, they are such slow starters. They are very difficult to arouse, and when it comes to new ideas imported from elsewhere, especially from across the Atlantic, their instinctive reaction is negative. Cautious, they call it. To the more quickly stirred they are infuriatingly phlegmatic, standing aloof in a slightly patronising manner like adults looking on at a display of childish enthusiasm. It takes a lot to move them and although, once started, they can usually be depended upon to keep going, they keep going in their own way. It is not that they deliberately break the rules – they merely ignore them. The irate general who, having just won a decisive battle, discovered that the British were still fighting, summed up this characteristic when he said, "The English never know when they're beaten." It is a tendency of theirs doggedly to pursue their own course, irrespective of events.

So what with one thing and another, "You need to understand the British," the American Gideons agreed, wondering uneasily whether, in fact, they did. "If we're going to establish Gideon work over there, we'll have to do it the British way."

But what was the British way? The American Gideons could not define it, and looked challengingly at the Canadian Gideons who, they felt, were in a better position to do so. After all, Canada had been British much more recently than America.

Away back in 1911, when Canada was British, The Gideons in Chicago had received a letter from Canada cheerfully announcing that an association of Christian commercial travellers had been started there, calling itself

The Gideons of Canada. It had caused quite a stir at the time, and the American Gideons had promptly copyrighted their title and emblem to ensure that sort of thing did not happen again.

That was all in the past, of course, the two organisations had amalgamated and now, with representatives from both countries on The Gideon International Extension Committee, they worked as one. When it came to getting The Gideons started in Great Britain, therefore, it was agreed that a Canadian would stand a better chance of succeeding than an American. With the blessing of the Committee, a Canadian went to Great Britain with the object of establishing work in that country.

Some time later he returned to give his report. Naturally, it was quite a full one, but put in a nutshell he had to admit that he had failed. The gist of what he said was simply this: "You'll never get Gideons going over there unless it's started by one of themselves."

Dampened but undaunted, the Committee applied itself to finding a Briton to introduce The Gideons into Britain in the British way. The Canadian Gideon was not without ideas on the subject. He had met several organisations that were sympathetic and ready to help if they could, one of which was the Scripture Gift Mission (SGM). It was a very unassuming society, with its modest headquarters in an old-fashioned building near Victoria Station, but he had been impressed by what he saw of the extent of their work, producing Scripture portions in hundreds of languages for free distribution all over the world. They got things done in a thoroughly businesslike way, and had an area secretary who was promoting the work in Britain. This area secretary had contacts all over the country, and if he could be seconded to The Gideons for a period of two or three years, there was a good chance of the association getting established there. "In a way they are engaged in a similar type of activity to ours, and understand our aims."

And so it came about that some time in 1948 The Gideons International in Chicago welcomed into their midst a Mr. Montague H. Knott of London, England. He had come at their invitation, seconded by the SGM, to spend a few months in the USA and Canada, to see how the Gideon organisation worked, and to meet as many as possible of The Gideons themselves.

Mr. Montague H. Knott (Monty to his friends) was a personable young man who looked the part of a well-dressed Englishman even in suits that had seen several years' wear. His American hosts had no idea of the time he'd had of it getting his wardrobe together. The Second World War was over, but Britain was still in the dull aftermath of the blockade that had resulted in the rationing of clothing as well as of food. So many points for a shirt, so many points for a pair of shoes, and if you decided on a new suit you gave up all idea of getting a raincoat. Like everyone else, he'd been juggling with his ration books for years.

If the vast range of suits and shirts and flamboyant ties the Americans could buy in unlimited quantities took him by surprise he managed not to show it, but he was not so successful in concealing his amazement when it came to food. The very sight of the juicy steaks and the tasty sea foods, the luscious salads and the cream cakes, the fruit and the nuts, all in such abundance and no ration books required, fairly took his breath away. It was like walking backwards through Joseph's interpretation of Pharaoh's dream, from the years of famine into the years of plenty. The blazing lights, the flow of limousines, the spontaneity and the generosity plunged him into another world, a sort of real-life Disneyland. And as the North American Gideons seemed to enjoy sharing all their good things with their guest, he was healthy enough and honest enough to admit that he was having the time of his life.

There was something else about those Gideons of North America, though, that impressed him. They were always on the job, The Gideons' job of standing up and speaking up for what they believed – when they were planning how to reach the areas where there were still hotels without Bibles, or when they made their presentations in prisons, or went off to visit someone who had written in wanting spiritual help after being unexpectedly confronted with a Bible in the motel where he'd put up for the night. In such circumstances it was to be expected that they would speak about God and Jesus Christ – and also at the banquets they put on to recruit new members.

Monty was slightly awed when he first heard that a banquet was to be held, conjuring up pictures of the sort of thing he'd heard about at Buckingham Palace or the Guildhall. It was rather a relief to find that it wasn't quite like that, that it wasn't a "white bow and tails" affair, and that there were no footmen in uniform to hand round the dishes. All the same it was quite stately, held in one of the best hotels, and although no wines were served the soft drinks were of the highest quality, and the food first rate. No expense had been spared, that was evident.

The men who had been invited, business executives accustomed to entertaining prospective clients on a lavish scale, were quite at home in such an atmosphere. And since they were all church-goers, and knew what to expect at a Gideon banquet, no one was surprised that the speakers emphasised the Christian's responsibility to proclaim to all and sundry the way of eternal salvation through faith in Jesus Christ, and offered membership in The Gideons as a means of fulfilling it. A number of them joined then and there.

"This is our usual method of recruiting," he was told. "Though we do it personally, of course, when we meet someone suitable in the course of our daily business." But recruiting members for The Gideons was not their primary concern. Monty noticed the way they introduced spiritual matters into ordinary casual conversations. It was likely to happen anywhere, he found – in the train, in a restaurant, at a social function. One never knew when one's companions would have passed from a few desultory remarks to an earnest presentation of basic facts about man's spiritual need and God's method of meeting it, and all to a complete stranger. It was the sort of situation that would have caused the average Englishman, as an onlooker, the most acute embarrassment, and Monty

sometimes found himself wondering how the individual
concerned would react. He was surprised how often the
response was appreciative, even eager, as though a hidden
tension was finding relief. Perhaps more people were
ready to listen to talk about weighty matters of judgment
and forgiveness than he had realised. Perhaps there were
some who were unconsciously even longing for it.

"Aggressive personal evangelism of the character
practised in the USA and Canada is not common in
European countries," he wrote later. He had been
challenged by what he had heard and seen. "One feels
that... this aspect of the work should be promoted."

The highlight of his visit to North America was The
Gideons' Golden Anniversary held for five days in July
1949. Nearly 2,000 people gathered from all over North
America and even some from the Scandinavian countries,
including twenty-eight who arrived together from Sweden
and received a special ovation from the whole assembly.
By the time Monty returned to England he was full of
enthusiasm for his new task, and, having established
himself in an office, he set about launching The Gideons
in Great Britain.

It must start, of course, with a banquet.

Just how to put on a Gideon banquet which would be
appreciated in Britain involved him in some thought and
consultation. Would not a luncheon be more appropriate?
Yes, definitely! Obviously, it couldn't be held in a church
hall or the YMCA, but on the other hand a hotel in Park
Lane or the Strand wouldn't be suitable, either. In the end
he decided on a hotel in Bloomsbury. Then he sent out
invitations to the business men he'd been in touch with
about it, and one day in November 1949 some fifty of them
sat down in the Marlborough Room of the Bonnington to
a four-course luncheon, British style, starting with soup
and ending with cheese, to hear what The Gideons
International was, what were its aims, and what were the
privileges and responsibilities of those who were enrolled
as members.

It was a layman's organisation, they were told, an

association of Christian business men whose object was to win men and women for the Lord Jesus Christ, not only by their personal testimony, but also by placing Bibles or New Testaments in hotels, hospitals, schools and prisons. For this privilege they paid an annual subscription and were expected to be ready, when called upon, to undertake the journeys and interviews which were involved in this form of Bible distribution.

But what a privilege it was! Monty spoke, the American Gideon who had come over specially for the occasion spoke, and what tales they had to tell of people whose lives had been changed through reading the Bibles they had found on their bedside tables, the evidence they could produce of the effectiveness of this widespread activity! The British might be slow to respond to new opportunities and fresh challenges, but some of them, at any rate, rose to the occasion that day. Amongst them was Frederick W. Bradbury. Along with a dozen or so others he joined The Gideons at once.

He was a civil servant, he explained, a senior official at the GPO Sorting Office at Mount Pleasant just a few minutes' walk away. When The Gideons' headquarters was moved to John Street, WC1, he immediately offered his services. If there was any way in which he could assist there, let Monty call on him. He'd be delighted to lend a hand at anything – packing Bibles, keeping accounts, filing. And when it came to offering the managers of local hotels supplies of Gideon Bibles to be placed in all the bedrooms, he'd be willing to do that too.

Monty took him at his word. A lot more correspondence was coming to Monty's desk, and many more visitors to his office than he had bargained for. The International Extension Committee, heavily involved in its programme of introducing Gideons to Christian business men abroad, was finding it very convenient to have a representative in London who could deal with affairs on the continent of Europe. The office in John Street became quite a centre for Scandinavian Gideons to refer to and to visit when in Britain, and when Monty took his first annual report to

Chicago it included memoranda on Sweden, Norway, Finland, Holland and South Africa.

On Germany, he reported: "Apparently an association of Christian business men existed in this country for many years prior to the Hitler regime. When Hitler came to power it was suppressed and now a move to re-form the association has begun. The brethren in Sweden first made contact and discovered an interest on the part of the Germans to relate themselves to The Gideons International... I have followed up this original contact through the post."

It was fortunate for Monty that Fred Bradbury's own office at Mount Pleasant was so easily accessible. It was even more fortunate that he was coming up for retirement. By September 1950, when Monty had arranged to go to Ireland for three weeks, Fred Bradbury was ready to man the office in his absence on a full-time basis.

The burly retired civil servant proved to be a man with a great deal to offer, whose career in the apparently unromantic environment of a GPO sorting office had been enlivened by emergencies brought about by two world wars. There had been occasions when highly important missives of a strictly confidential nature had been entrusted to his care, and he had been shipped off to deliver them personally to generals in various places on the far-flung battle line. It sounded like a cross between a king's Messenger and a Secret Service agent, and although Brother Fred was careful not to divulge anything that would contravene the Official Secrets Act, he came out sometimes with reminiscences of his own personal adventures.

As for his work on the home front, he had come in for special recognition for the way he had kept the mail moving from Mount Pleasant all through the bombings and the Blitz. He took a boyish pleasure in displaying the two medals he had received.

But none of it could compare with the thrilling task that was opening up to him now. He was in his element entertaining the Gideons who dropped in to the office from all sorts of places. He went off eagerly to speak at meetings about the transforming power of the Word of God in human lives, and how The Gideons were engaged in spreading it. Even the routine work in the office delighted him. The room he shared with Monty was on the second floor, the reception desk and the typists on the ground floor and the store rooms in the basement. Upstairs, downstairs, a dozen times a day could not dull his enthusiasm, nor even the slowness with which members were enrolled and branches started. Just at what point his natural optimism ended and his quiet faith began it would be difficult to say, but his conviction that God was going to get The Gideons established and thriving in Great Britain seemed never to waver. It impelled him to undertake tasks from which he would otherwise have shrunk.

"I wonder if you can enter into my feelings when, in the course of trying to place Bibles in hotel bedrooms, I stood outside such a world-famous hotel as the Hotel Cecil," he wrote years later. "The elite of the world doing business in London stayed in this hotel. Standing outside I prayed for courage to enter the building and talk to the managing director in seeking permission to place Bibles in the bedrooms. I confess to feelings of much fear and trembling, but with the help of the Lord I obtained an interview with the general manager only to find that the Lord had gone before me and that the manager had travelled in America and seen Gideon Bibles in hotel bedrooms. He received me very courteously, listened to my request, and instantly agreed to have Bibles placed in every bedroom of his hotel."

Fred Bradbury was encouraged. "Thank God!" he thought. "Here is a major breakthrough! Now I can go to other lesser hotels in the city of London and tell them that the Hotel Cecil has Bibles. It's sure to make an impact, and they'll be glad to follow suit." With great confidence he walked a short distance along the Strand to another well-known hotel to make the same request. To his dismay, he met with a very different reception here, and within a short time was out in the street again. "Never shall I forget the disappointment as I left that hotel having been rebuffed and refused."

Nor were they alone in their refusal. English hoteliers were none too eager to risk the effect on patrons at finding Bibles by their bedsides. They might not like it.

There was as much to discourage The Gideons as there was to enthuse in those early years. Membership did not increase to the extent that had been hoped, and the first flush of interest soon died down, especially when it became apparent that there were regulations and forms of procedure that members were expected to observe. A number who had joined did not renew their subscriptions, and by July 1952 the annual report sent to Chicago could tell of only 412 Gideons on the British list – and forty-nine of them were overseas.

However, if things were going slowly in Great Britain, they were going better in the Scandinavian countries, and for Fred Bradbury one of the most stimulating experiences of his whole career was to attend, with Monty, the Gideon Convention in Stockholm. It was the first of its kind to be held in Europe, and as Gideons from eight countries gathered in the foyer of the Hotel Malmen there was a good deal of laughter and gesticulating when they tried, with varying success, to talk each other's language.

Fred Bradbury revelled in it all. The visit to Swedish homes, the leisureliness of the meals – an insurance against the dyspepsia troubling so many in the English-speaking countries, laughed Monty – the reception in the Town Hall when a message from the Prime Minister commending the Gideon movement was read out, the after-church coffee served in the famous Gold Hall, the meetings and the Bible readings, the reports and the testimonies, he took it all in his stride. Most moving of all, perhaps, was an incident that took place at the final meeting, when two Gideons from Denmark and Norway, countries that had suffered bitterly under the Nazis during the war, shook hands warmly with the one German Gideon who had come to the Convention.

That convention was almost the last time he and Monty travelled together. Monty's time with The Gideons was drawing to a close, and he was getting ready to enter theological college in preparation for ordination in the Church of England. The position he had held as secretary to The Gideons International in the British Isles fell vacant, and there was only one person who seemed fitted to fill the post – Fred Bradbury, retired official from a GPO sorting office.

4 Getting Established

Salesmanship is an invaluable asset in the modern world. Diligent labour and the manufacture of reliable goods are not all that is required for prosperity. Someone has to introduce the products, and convince potential customers that they will be immeasurably benefited by possessing them.

The same principle applies in other realms, and when it came to getting the Gideon movement into Britain, salesmanship was required. Christian men who were executives in the workaday world of twentieth-century trade had to be persuaded that a sort of evangelistic club was just what they were looking for, and that it was to be found in The Gideons.

The time was ripe for such an organisation. The country was recovering at last from the after-effects of the war. Commercial air travel was widening the horizons of business men, many of whom had noticed with some surprise that Bibles bearing the Gideon emblem were to be seen in the bedrooms of nearly all the hotels in North America where they stayed. The superficial interest that this had aroused was ready to be quickened.

There was generally a greater underlying concern about spiritual matters than was realised in those early years of the 1950s. This was manifested at the Greater London Crusade when, contrary to the *Daily Mirror*'s prediction that the unknown American evangelist Billy Graham would not fill the Harringay stadium for so much as one night, he succeeded in doing so for three months, preaching both judgment and forgiveness with an open Bible in his hand. Thoughtful, intelligent laymen in the prime of life were becoming aware that opportunities for personal evangelism beyond the reach of the clergy lay within their grasp, but they did not know how to grasp them. The Gideons could provide them with the very help they were looking for.

Fred Bradbury seemed to have all the right characteristics for putting these men in touch with The Gideons. Brother Fred, as he came to be known, was the possessor of a friendly disposition and a gregarious nature, to which were added business ability, an eloquent tongue, and his unbounded enthusiasm for anything he undertook. Public speaking was quite in his line. He'd been doing it for years. Not only on Sundays but on week nights too he was likely to be off preaching somewhere, as well as shouldering his responsibilities as an elder of the church to which he belonged. His spare time was entirely taken up with some activity or other connected with what he called "the service of the King of kings".

Now that he was national secretary for The Gideons in the British Isles it was full-time service, and nothing could have delighted him more. He was in business for God. The particular job assigned to him was to enlist as many Christian business men as possible, form them into branches, and encourage them to meet regularly to arrange for systematic distribution of Bibles. The real aim of this distribution was to lead people to faith in Jesus Christ.

He gave his whole attention to it. His wife, Amy by name and amiable by nature, rarely knew when to expect him home. He was constantly on the move. Visits to clergymen to explain The Gideons' structure and ask for names of suitable business men in their congregations who could be approached, then back to the office to write letters. More interviews, speaking at meetings, and back to the office to write more letters.

And if there was the likelihood of starting a branch he would be off to Land's End or John o'Groats or anywhere in between. To start a local branch was a main objective. He admitted his eagerness to achieve it. He could chuckle over his own enthusiasm, laugh over the mistakes he made, and tell a story against himself to illustrate his tendency to jump ahead too quickly.

One of those stories concerned the establishing of a branch in the north of England. An encouraging invitation was received from an influential man in one of the cities to come and spend a few days and see what could be done. Brother Fred responded with alacrity. His host was a live wire who knew many of the local Christian business men, and within a short time invitations had been issued for a luncheon party at a certain hotel to hear about The Gideons.

On the day appointed Brother Fred went along early to finalise arrangements and particularly to ensure that the large round table he had selected in the dining-room was marked "Reserved". He had a word with the manager as well as the head waiter about it. Only those who had been invited to the Gideon luncheon party were to be directed to it. Others must be steered elsewhere. And as he wanted to be free to talk when his guests arrived, he would have his meal served a little ahead of time.

He had barely commenced eating when, to his dismay, a smartly dressed man walked straight across the dining-room with a confident air, sat down beside him, and reached for the menu. A waiter immediately appeared at his elbow, to whom Brother Fred shot frantic though covert glances, in a fruitless effort to gain his attention. The waiter ignored him completely, standing pad in hand ready to take the newcomer's orders with an obsequious "Yes sir... no sir... certainly sir". Then he turned on his heel and hurried off, evidently intent on fulfilling as promptly as he could, the order he had been given.

Brother Fred was in a dilemma. Should he go off and find the manager to complain that his instructions had not been carried out? Should he explain to the man himself that this table was reserved? Or should he just let things take their course? Before he could make up his mind the man turned to him and started a conversation.

"Are you a visitor to our city or do you live here?" he asked in a friendly manner. Courtesy demanded a polite reply.

"No, I don't live here – I'm here on a short visit."

"And are you here on business or on pleasure?"

"Well, you might say I'm here on both," replied Brother Fred. "Because my business *is* my pleasure."

His companion smiled. "And what is your business?" he enquired.

"It's a little difficult to explain. I'm really here on business for God."

Rather to his surprise the man said quite calmly, "I, too. I go to a number of functions, Church anniversaries and so on, in the course of my office. I happen to be the Mayor, and I feel it my duty to encourage religion in this city."

Brother Fred was greatly elated by this revelation. It did not occur to him to respond to his companion's overtures by asking a few polite questions about himself. All he could think of was what it would mean if this important man became interested in The Gideons. His agile mind leapt ahead, picturing future gatherings in which the Mayor graced the occasion with his presence. He may have thought it would be at least a step towards measuring up to the Swedish Gideons, with their public recognition by the Prime Minister at the Convention in Stockholm. While his companion ate, Brother Fred told him about the movement – but even as he talked he was thinking about the men who would soon be arriving for the luncheon, and suddenly an idea struck him. Why not ask the manager if Gideons could place Bibles in this very hotel? What zest would be added to what he had to say if he could tell them that permission had already been granted for the first Bible placement right here!

He pushed back his chair. "Excuse me," he said, and scrambled to his feet. "I just want to have a word with the manager."

When he returned, the Mayor had finished his meal and was preparing to depart. Brother Fred beamed on him and shared his good news.

"I've just been to ask the manager if we may place Bibles in this hotel," he said. "Isn't it splendid! He's agreed. Certainly we may place Bibles here, he says. He'll be glad to make arrangements for the presentation in due

course." The Mayor was unimpressed. "You need not
have bothered to ask the manager," he said casually. Then
he added a simple statement which explained all that had
gone before.

"I own this hotel," he said.

Brother Fred had a sense of the dramatic, and when he
told a story he knew where to stop. He usually stopped
there, long enough to enjoy the chuckles of his audience
before assuring them that the outcome of his visit to that
city was the formation of a vigorous branch there.

He was not so successful everywhere. In another north
of England city there was plenty of interest shown at the
carefully planned luncheon, and all appeared to be going
well until it became clear that two or three of the most
vocal in the group had ideas of their own as to how things
should be done. Getting Bibles placed in hotels and
schools was a simple matter, they said. They'd been in
Christian work for years, so it was the sort of activity that
they were accustomed to. No need to form a local branch of
The Gideons with fees to be paid, meetings to attend, and
formalities regarding the placing of Bibles to be observed.
"Give us the Bibles and we'll distribute them for you, free
of charge, and that'll be the end of it."

In vain Brother Fred pointed out that the Gideon
movement involved far more than the placing of Bibles in
various institutions. It was also for fellowship among like-
minded men of business, for mutual encouragement and
help in the commission they had all received to proclaim
to everyone that Christ Jesus came into the world to save
sinners – not to condemn them. A widening network was
being formed whereby Gideons, not only in this country,
but abroad as well, could recognise each other and work
together towards getting this message to individuals in the
main traffic lanes of the modern world. The placing of
Bibles was only one aspect of the Gideon movement, not
even the most important.

His arguments and explanations may have convinced
some of the quieter men present, but the more vocal were
unimpressed. They saw no reason for the club aspect of

The Gideons, with its badge and its terms of membership. The local distribution of Bibles is what caught their imagination. They were eager enough to do that, but they wanted to do it as individuals in their own way. Working as a team along prescribed lines had no appeal for them. When Brother Fred left he had recruited a few new members, but not enough to form a local branch, as he had hoped. He'd try again, later.

Meanwhile, there was plenty going on in the branches that had already been formed. The first one had been in Portsmouth, where Fred and Monty had gone to meet a group of men in a café. On their return to London, they formed the second one on the Essex border, where they themselves both lived. "And so it continued to go on, branch after branch being formed wherever six members could be recruited." Brother Fred was in his element now, happier than he had ever been.

"Looking back I marvel at the amount of work which passed through the office and how the Lord used the small staff of one man, one typist and one general assistant working in a small inconvenient office, with the secretary away two or three days each week, travelling throughout the British Isles. This often involved travelling all night, writing all day, coming back with a bag full of letters already written out for the typist, and then dealing with questions of policy and other matters, including the accounts."

... Not to mention all the background work connected with the placing of Bibles.

The enthusiasm to get on with the Bible distribution had encountered an unexpected obstacle in the early days of The Gideons in Britain. Arrangements were going ahead very smoothly for an importation of Gideon Bibles from the USA, when a letter arrived at the office in John Street one day from no less a person than the holder of the King's copyright. So the Bible was copyright? It came as quite a shock to learn that the King James version, commonly known as the Authorised Version, certainly was, and The Gideons' secretary was informed with crisp courtesy that he was not permitted to import Bibles in that version from America. It caused quite a commotion at the time, involving explorations into the world of printing and publishing, but after various tenders had been sent out and samples scrutinised, the day came when they handled with pride and satisfaction the first Bible printed in Britain bearing the Gideon emblem and containing the Gideon introductory notes.

The business details of publishing Bibles and New Testaments gradually became a matter of office routine, but there were some things which were beyond Brother Fred. For instance, there was the special opportunity afforded by the coronation of Queen Elizabeth II. A business executive accustomed to looking ahead and planning on a large scale was the right person to tackle this, and it was one of the many occasions when the value of team work became evident.

C. Alexander Clark, managing director of Caribonum, had been on the British Council of The Gideons from its inception. His fertile brain was not lacking in practical ideas for the advancement of the organisation, nor an intuitive sense of the ripeness of time. The forthcoming coronation of the young Queen was a matter not only of national importance, but of international interest. The tourist trade would be booming and the hotels full. This was the time for The Gideons to make a nationwide approach to them all with their offer of a Bible for each room, complete with a special bookmark to commemorate the event. It would be a singularly appropriate thing to have on display, for the presentation of a Bible to the sovereign was an indispensable part of the coronation ceremony in Westminster Abbey.

The opportunity, as Alec Clark saw it, was too good to be missed, and with some thirty area branches now established throughout the British Isles, he was convinced The Gideons could reach every hotel in the country. There seemed to be only one serious obstacle to be overcome, but that was a formidable one. He reckoned that about 50,000 Bibles would be required, and the order for them ought to be put in hand immediately if they were to be ready in time.

The question was, where was the money to come from to pay for them? The local branches could not raise it, that was certain, and they had no other resources. He discussed it with the council members, and eventually they agreed that the parent organisation in America should be approached. In view of all it was providing already to maintain the British work it was with some hesitation that they decided to ask for further help, but there was nothing else for it. Alec Clark agreed to write to the International Cabinet in Chicago, outlining the ideas the British Gideons had on how to get Bibles placed in every hotel in the country during coronation year, and stating frankly that they had not got the money for the 50,000 Bibles they reckoned would be necessary for the distribution.

A few days after he had dispatched the letter, the telephone rang in his home. It was a transatlantic call from Chicago, and the wires fairly tingled with the excitement in the voice at the other end. It was Dirk De Pree, president of the American Gideons.

"Brother, the Lord is in this! At our Cabinet meeting we had been talking about coronation year in Britain, wondering what could be done about it, when your letter arrived. Just at that time! It was an answer to our prayers. This is just to let you know that we will provide all the dollars necessary for those 50,000 copies. Go ahead and put the order in. We're in this with you. The Lord bless you!"

So Alec Clark went ahead. Putting in the order for 50,000 Bibles took him far less time than providing the special book marks to go with them. The 1,200 employees of Caribonum would have been mildly surprised if they could have seen how their managing director spent his evenings when at home. Thousands of yards of red, white and blue ribbon had to be cut into three-inch lengths to which ornamental labels, commemorating the coronation and giving helpful suggestions about Bible reading, had to be neatly affixed. He organised teams of volunteers to help him do the job, and he had the bookmarks ready in time for the local branches to move into action.

It was the biggest distribution The Gideons had ever undertaken in Britain, and some of them spent a good deal of time and money travelling to distant places to reach the hotels beyond their own vicinities. But hoteliers, by and large, responded warmly to the offer made to them. Very few rejected it. Bibles in bedrooms to commemorate the event that was bringing them so many visitors from overseas would provide an additional touch of distinction to the decor. "Free of charge?" they asked with surprise. "That's very generous of you!" And that gave The Gideons the opportunity to explain briefly why they did it.

By the end of coronation year 55,000 Bibles had been placed in hotels throughout the length and breadth of the British Isles. Travellers and tourists were becoming vaguely aware of an organisation called The Gideons. "They're the Bible people, aren't they?" From the point of view of the man of commerce, it was all good for business.

Outwardly things were going well, and from various sources came evidence of the value of the Bible distribution. Brother Fred was the recipient of most of these, and he made good use of them. He told of the bright-faced young man who had walked into his office one day and explained quite frankly that he had just been released after serving a prison sentence in Wormwood Scrubs. He was now on his way back to Scotland, but had called in at the Gideon office first because he had something to tell them. While in prison he'd looked into one of the Bibles they had placed in the cells, and found himself believing what he read there. He'd gone on reading in spite of the jeers of fellow prisoners, and eventually he'd got down on his knees and asked God to take him on. Now he was on his way home to start a new life, with the Spirit of Christ in his heart.

"What a thrill it was to kneel in the office with that young man and pray together to the Lord who had died for us both!" said Brother Fred, his face aglow. Then he went on to tell how he had offered the young man a Bible so that he could go on reading, but had received the reply, "Don't worry, sir, I've already got one. When I left prison they gave me the things I had when I went in, also a small sum of money, and I came out of prison and the first shop I noticed was a second-hand bookshop, so I went in and asked if they had a second-hand Bible. They had and I bought it. Here it is."

Then there was the dignified-looking man who had walked into the office one day saying he'd come to buy a Bible. "I'm sorry, sir," Brother Fred had said politely. "They're not for sale."

"I want a Gideon Bible," said the man firmly. "I saw one in the hotel where I was staying and was very impressed by it. I'll make a donation to the society." And sitting down he drew out his cheque book and wrote one for £10. "I want a Gideon Bible."

In the face of such determination Brother Fred could do no other than let him have one. It was not until he looked at the signature on the cheque and saw the name Adrian Boult on it that he realised he was talking to the most celebrated orchestral conductor of the day.

There were other less spectacular but equally encouraging encounters from the Bible distribution in hospitals, hotels and schools as well. Brother Fred had plenty of stories to tell at the various meetings at which he spoke. The Bible was doing its unique work in hotel bedrooms and prison cells, on hospital lockers and in schoolchildren's desks, waiting patiently, as it were, for one or another of the heedless passers-by to stop and listen to its message.

Yes, things appeared to be going well in the British branch of The Gideons. The rank and file of the members were enthusiastically holding their monthly meetings and reporting on Bibles placed, funds raised, new members recruited. Avenues of service for their Master were opening up that had been undreamed of before.

Few of them were aware of the storm that was brewing, nor, for that matter, were most of the members of the national council. Only one of them saw where the organisation was heading and that, like a ship that had got off course, it was in danger of being broken on the rocks.

5   Constitutional Crisis

The assembly hall of Durham Prison was in an uproar. It all happened so suddenly and simultaneously that the warders, as well as the group of men on the platform, were taken by surprise. The opening remarks of the chaplain had sparked it off as, with a beaming smile he had announced,

"Well, men, it's happened. I've been telling you that The Gideons were coming and here..." The rest of his sentence was drowned as one wit raised his voice in a refrain that was taken up immediately by hundreds of others,

> The Gideons are coming, hurrah! Hurrah!
> The Gideons are coming, hurrah! Hurrah!
> The Gideons are coming to bonnie old Durham
> The Gideons are coming, hurrah! Hurrah!

If the adjective shouted was not "bonnie" in every case, but came into the category referred to at that time as unprintable, it was all very good humoured and the warders grinned while the men on the platform, Brother Fred among them, took stock of their surroundings and prepared to go into action.

It was a favourite story of his, that visit to Durham Prison, one made very early in his years as secretary to The Gideons. Always aware of the mood of his listeners, he sensed the pleasure of temporary relief from the monotony of prison life, and glowed at the prospect of telling these men of the liberating power of Jesus Christ. In all his years of preaching to orderly congregations in Christian Brethren halls, he had rarely experienced the thrill he got as he looked over that sea of masculine faces, knowing he had heartening words for those who had fallen foul of the law, and Bibles to leave with them.

If anything, the chaplain was even more excited. The arrival of this little team of ordinary business men – not a dog-collar among them – with their unaffected manner and everyday appearance substantiated all he had been saying about them. They had come with a huge consignment of Bibles, sufficient for one to be placed in each cell, and they weren't receiving a penny. On the contrary, they were paying for the privilege. They had not only met all their own expenses in getting here, but they'd contributed towards the cost of the Bibles as well. No one could say they were doing the job because they were paid for it – a comment often made about the clergy. Now here they were, prepared to say why they were doing it, and the prisoners were prepared to listen.

The meeting went well. There was a cheerful atmosphere, the singing went with a swing, and when the time came for the speakers there was an attentive silence. The chaplain knew that among that vast concourse of men, hearts were being touched and consciences quickened. This visit of The Gideons was providing just the sort of opportunity that was needed to drive home the message he had been trying to convey during past months.

He was profoundly grateful to The Gideons, not only for the Bibles they were providing, but for their coming in person to deliver them. It did not end there. When the meeting was over, and some of the prisoners indicated rather furtively, for fear of being laughed at by the others, that they wanted to hear more, The Gideons were in no hurry to leave. They had all the time in the world, they implied, to stop and talk.

If the chaplain had felt he was battling on alone before, he felt it no longer. The Gideons were behind him, evidently as concerned as he was about those men who had talked to them privately, wanting to know how they were getting on, and sharing his satisfaction when some of them gave evidence of a change of disposition that was undoubtedly for the better. So when one of the prisoners was drawing near to the end of his sentence, and faced the prospect of trying to find a job with the stigma of gaol against him, the chaplain knew where to turn. He could vouch for the sincerity of this man's faith – could The Gideons do anything to help him at this time of crisis?

The Gideons could and did. One of them owned a factory, and took the man into his employment, and saw him established as a citizen and a Christian.

"And that's the way The Gideons work," Brother Fred would say when he explained how from first to last it had been a team effort, from the arrangement made between the Newcastle Gideon and the chaplain to place Bibles in Durham prison, to the re-establishing to normal life of that man. And if the story lost nothing in the telling, and was rounded off by such words as,

> At the close of the day
> 'Twill be sweet to say,
> We have brought some lost one home,

well, that was Brother Fred's way, as those who knew him best understood. The Gideon council members, chairing the well organised luncheons or dinners at which Fred spoke, became accustomed to seeing the eyes of practical, down-to-earth business men kindle in response to his ardour, and their hands reach out for the application forms, eager to enrol as members on the spot.

"Don't sign now," the cautious chairmen would say, remembering occasions when enthusiasm had waned with morning light, and letters had been received withdrawing what had been agreed to at that inspiring meal. "Go home and pray about it for a day or two, then if you believe God is leading you to join, send us your application." Only those who meant what they said, and were prepared to act on it, were wanted in The Gideons.

The Durham Prison story was only one of those in Brother Fred's repertoire. Another that he enjoyed relating, especially at Auxiliary meetings for the wives of Gideons, was the case of the Frenchwoman who landed up in Holloway Prison in London. Bibles had been placed there, and one day a letter arrived at The Gideons' office from a wardress. She told of the way the French prisoner was devouring the Bible, and was visibly affected by what she read. The reason for the wardress' approach to The Gideons was that the prisoner was to be sent back to France, and had expressed the fear that there would be no Bible in the cell she would occupy in Paris. Could The Gideons help?

There was no Gideon branch in France at the time, so it took quite a lot of background work and an approach through the right channels to get a Bible into that cell, but eventually it was accomplished and, as later reports indicated, with the best of results.

Something else happened, too. Brother Fred went to Paris, and a Gideon branch was started there. The International Committee in Chicago took note of The Gideons' secretary in Great Britain. He was getting things done. The regular reports he sent in were full of information about progress made, and The Gideons in America, practical business men that they were, were assured that the money they were pouring into the British work was being well spent. "It's the Lord's money we're administering," was their attitude, and they kept a close eye on it, just as in their own businesses. And just as they took note of an employee who did his job well, so they noticed Brother Fred. They invited him over to America to report in person, and off he went, slightly subdued at first to find himself moving in the affluent stream of American business executives, but unable to restrain his exuberance when it came to telling how God was working through The Gideons in Britain, and what opportunities were opening up before them.

The American Gideons warmed to him. Their founder John Nicholson, had been just such an enthusiast. He seemed to understand them, too, to appreciate the methods they employed. Those visits he made to the States were to prove of far greater importance than appeared at the time, for it was then that he gained his insight into the value of discipline and also of restrictions in such an organisation as The Gideons. That insight stood him in good stead when the storm broke that threatened to finish The Gideons in Britain, and which certainly split that apparently flourishing organisation in two.

Although things did not come to a head until the annual convention in 1956, trouble had been brewing for three or four years. Conflicting personalities with strong convictions inevitably figured in the war of words that waged during that time, but the basic cause of the contention was the constitution.

A good deal of trouble sprang from misunderstandings as to what constituted a minister of a church and what did not. Many of the British Gideons belonged to the denomination known as the Christian Brethren, about which the North American Gideons had heard little and knew less. The Christian Brethren disclaimed having an ordained ministry, while The Gideons of North America knew of no church without one.

"Who are these men?" they queried. "They are Bible-believing Christians, certainly, but are they ministers? They act and speak as though they are the ministers of their own churches, but stoutly deny being anything of the sort. Some of them don't even admit to being members – stick to the idea that they are just 'in fellowship'." And since the Gideon movement had always been composed of laymen who could prove that they were church members in good standing with their ministers, the International Cabinet was none too easy about the way the British work was developing.

The National Council in Britain, on the other hand, was coming to the conclusion that the constitution as passed in 1952 was too restrictive. These rules and regulations left no room for the Spirit to work, they argued. The rule that no national officer could hold office for more than three consecutive years, for instance. If a man obviously had God-given gifts for a position, why should a man-made regulation preclude him from exercising it for an indefinite period? It ought to be changed.

There were other matters, too. A lively correspondence kept the various issues before the minds of the councils on both sides of the Atlantic, and if Brother Fred was uneasy at the way things were going, Alec Clark was even more so. He was in the unenviable position of being a lone voice on the British National Council as he argued for the right of The Gideons International, based in Chicago, to agree the constitution. It was not merely the age-old contention that the payer, not the player, is the one to call the tune. No one was in any doubt as to where the large proportion of financial support for the British Gideons was coming from – from the International Cabinet. But there was more to it than that. Their policies had been thrashed out in the light of the fifty-years experience they had behind them.

"The Gideons International was already an established organisation when it was introduced here in Britain. We have joined them, they haven't joined us. It is for us to abide by the rules they have made, not to try to change them."

The British Council did not agree with him. One or two of its members conceded that he had a point, and were dubious about the suggested rewording, for they saw the wider implications, but the voice of the majority won. The constitution was changed, though not without strong protests from the opposition in which The Gideons International in Chicago joined. The correspondence became even more animated, punctuated by trans-Atlantic phone calls, and eventually culminated in the arrival at the annual convention in 1956 of Stanley Boswell, a Canadian Gideon, sent as the representative of the International Committee, to deliver its ultimatum.

Boswell knew exactly what he had to say, and he said it. Unless the constitution reverted to its original form, as agreed by the International Cabinet, all financial help would be stopped, the British branch would be lopped off, and if it tried to continue under The Gideons' name and emblem, which had been patented, legal action would be taken to prevent its doing so.

That, in a nutshell, was the message he had come to deliver. The message was not received with quiet acquiescence. All that was said, though recorded at the time, was wisely not incorporated in the minutes.

There was a notable precedent for such an omission, mentioned in Acts 15. Paul the apostle and his close companion Barnabas had fallen out over whether or not young John Mark should be given a second chance and again be invited to accompany them on their missionary journeys. Barnabas said he should, Paul said he shouldn't. The Scriptures simply report: "There arose a sharp contention, so that they separated from each other."

Something of the sort happened now. Several Gideons had been nominated for the office of president, but none of them received a majority of votes. The convention broke up in some disarray, leaving the British Gideons not knowing quite where they were, but suspecting that it was nowhere at all. And as far as most of the members were concerned, there it could stay. They wanted no more to do with it. They crept off to bed, dismayed and disillusioned at the whole affair, eager only to return home at the crack of dawn, even if it did mean going without breakfast.

And that might have been the end of it had not Boswell, and what was left of the Council, sat up into the early hours of the morning, trying to find a way out of the impasse. By 1.30 a.m. they had decided what to do. Boswell rose to his feet, walked silently along the corridors of the hotel to Alec Clark's room, and knocked quietly but persistently at the door. It opened eventually to reveal him standing in his pyjamas, blinking the sleep out of his eyes and wondering why on earth he was being awakened at such an hour.

Boswell explained that he had come as spokesman for the meeting being held downstairs. "We want to ask you to be president of the British Gideons," he said.

If Alec Clark felt like groaning, he managed to conceal it, but it was no use pretending that he was keen on the idea. He had resigned from the Council some months before, and had just been through one of the most difficult experiences of his life. It is one thing to stand up against unbelievers for what you are convinced is right, but it is a very different matter to find yourself in opposition to those who are your brethren. He was in no mood to take on the responsibilities of president of a Council that was at sixes and sevens on fundamental matters, and said so.

"I won't even consider it unless they'll agree to my conditions," he said, and went on to say what they were.

"Fair enough," said Boswell. "Let's pray before we go down."

Not many words seemed necessary as the two of them knelt by the bed.

"Almighty God ... we commit the future to Thee. Give us Thy help, Thy guidance ... In Jesus' Name ..." Then they went downstairs, and Alec Clark gave his answer to the invitation to become president.

"I'll accept on two conditions," he said. "First, that *every* member of the Council agrees to accept the constitution and the rules already passed by the Cabinet of The Gideons International in Chicago, and that we abide by their regulations." He spelt it out carefully, so that there could be no mistakes made later. Only if there was unanimity on this point would he accept the presidency.

"Second, that everyone agrees to accept their share of the work, and not leave it all to me!" There was a slight easing of the tense solemnity of the atmosphere as he said that, though it was clear he meant it. Each man in turn gravely accepted the two conditions.

And each was as good as his word. A month later the new Council addressed a document to The Gideons International in Chicago, giving agreement to its policy and stating that its constitution "would be brought into conformity with International policy and practice." In September of that same year an Extraordinary General Meeting rectified the constitution, and the crisis was passed.

Brother Fred, heaving a sigh of relief, squared his shoulders. He was ready for action, and in the years that followed it was largely due to his efforts that The Gideons in Britain survived the storm it had encountered, and started forging ahead again.

It was a slow business. News of the split inevitably got through to the members, and many who did not actually resign failed to renew their subscriptions. Brother Fred had his work cut out visiting, phoning, writing to them, explaining the viewpoint of The Gideons International, and the necessity for uniformity in a worldwide organisation if it were to be effective in action, like a well disciplined army. He'd done so not without regret. One of the outcomes of the constitutional dispute had been for The Gideons International to decree "that the British Council should confine their interests to the British Isles, whilst Gideons in the USA would look after outside interests, including the British Commonwealth of nations."

This decision had hit Brother Fred rather hard at the time, for he had enjoyed meeting visitors from overseas to whom he could introduce The Gideons with a view to helping establish a branch in their countries. As things turned out, the restriction proved to be an advantage, for he was undistracted now in his task of getting the badly battered Gideon organisation in Britain in working order again.

Perhaps the most effective, and the most delicate activity to which he now turned his attention was the establishing of The Auxiliary. It proved to be the most effective because it mobilised the active and enthusiastic support of hundreds of women – and the most delicate for the very same reason.

Women! The Gideons was an exclusively masculine organisation. It did not enrol female colleagues, not even senior ones, into its membership. The wives of Gideons could be auxiliaries – this had been so in the British Isles since 1956 – but they had no status other than being the wives of Gideons. To them was entrusted the presentation of New Testaments to nurses, but that was all. Few of them ever attended the monthly meetings for prayer and planning which their husbands obviously found so stimulating. The praying they did was in private. They just made the coffee and produced the cakes at the appropriate time, and left the men to get on with it. And the British Gideons were content to have it so.

Not so the American Gideons. It was during one of his visits to the USA that it dawned on Brother Fred why the parent body was in such a thriving condition, always seemed to be on the go, never seemed to be short of money. Their wives were not merely the wives of Gideons – they were members of The Auxiliary.

The Auxiliary was the wives' organisation within The Gideons. Not that *any* Gideon's wife could join. Its basis of membership contained the same requirement of personal faith as that required of a Gideon. Without it she could not belong to The Auxiliary, so all the auxiliaries knew exactly where they stood. The Auxiliary had its own branches, its own meetings, and its own duly elected president. And from all Brother Fred saw of it in North America, members of The Auxiliary were as enthusiastic about their organisation as The Gideons were about theirs. They were in on the monthly meetings their husbands attended, often accompanied their husbands when presentations of Bibles were made, and when it came to following up women who wrote from hotels to Gideon headquarters, who better to do it than an auxiliary?

One way and another Brother Fred, who was very familiar with the Authorised Version of the Bible, realised that the creation of The Gideons was very similar to that referred to in Genesis 2 where it said, "And the Lord God said, 'It is not good that the man should be alone: I will make an help meet for him.'"

The American Gideons were a step ahead, there was no denying it. Brother Fred decided that it was high time the British Gideons tried to catch up. He knew he would have to proceed cautiously. It would not do to upset the more conservative of The Gideons, who saw the organisation as being exclusively male, and might eye with suspicion the idea of women being included. He knew the importance, too, not only of small beginnings but of right beginnings. The Auxiliary in the British Isles, if it were to be started at all, must be started right and with the right person.

The right person proved to be the wife of a prominent Lancashire Gideon. Brother Fred, who was in Southport on a visit, told of what he had seen women doing within The Gideons in America, of the thriving state of The Auxiliary there, and of his longing that something similar might be started in Britain. Mrs. J.M. Dalgleish was one of those fired by his enthusiasm, and she got to work. A little committee of four Gideon wives was formed to encourage others to talk in women's groups about The Gideons' Bible distribution, about what was happening as a result, to arrange meetings among themselves to pray and to plan. In short, she succeeded in quietly forming the hitherto unnoticed auxiliaries into The Auxiliary, while her husband and his supporters succeeded in putting it on the map – that is to say, on the agenda.

The British National Council of The Gideons International was forced to recognise that, since the auxiliaries had been taking a more active interest in the organisation, things had been looking up. The financial statements were healthier. Invitations to speak about the work were coming from hitherto unexplored sources, and opportunities for Bible distribution were growing, too. The facts were there, and could not be denied. The day came when The Auxiliary was officially recognised in the British Isles, at the annual convention in 1960, and in 1964 a further step was taken when The Auxiliary National Committee was formed, complete with its own president.

The Gideons would no doubt have appointed Mrs. J.M. Dalgleish into that position, but they had no say in the matter. The auxiliaries elected their own president. The fact that Mrs. J.M. Dalgleish was the one they elected all goes to prove how united in heart and mind were The Gideons and The Auxiliary. Which, of course, is just as it should be.

The process had taken some years to complete, but it started in the latter half of the 1950s, the period when The Gideons in the British Isles were getting back on their feet. Enthusiasm that had waned was reviving, with new members being recruited and area branches humming with eagerness to get on with the distribution of Bibles in local hotels, schools, hospitals and prisons. Their monthly meetings were animated affairs now, as one member and another came to them with reports of contacts that could be followed up.

"One of the members of my church is the religious education teacher in his school – he says he's sure his Head would welcome an approach from The Gideons. Yes, all right, I'll write to him . . ."

"My wife does voluntary work at the hospital, and has got to know the secretary. She says there would be no obstacle to Testaments being placed in the wards . . ."

"As Bible secretary I can report that I've visited all the hotels in our branch area, and all but three have agreed to have Bibles in the bedrooms. I've got the list here – now we must decide who can undertake the various presentations. . ."

So it went on. The Bibles were beginning to flow again. It was in this period that a Hampshire Gideon got in touch with the governor of Winchester gaol to see about Bibles being placed in the cells there. The move was to have far-reaching effects.

6   In Winchester Prison

The window in the cell let in the light quite well, but had
its limitations as an aperture through which to view the
world outside. All it revealed was the sky, and young Vic
Jackopson, remanded in custody until the Quarter
Sessions, soon got tired of looking at the blue dome of
heaven. He preferred something more down to earth, and
discovered that by standing on the little wooden table
thoughtfully provided by the authorities for the occupant
to sit at, he could see over the blank wall opposite to an
array of the roofs and chimneys of the ancient city of
Winchester. By craning his neck and peering downwards
he could even see the pavement of the courtyard below,
which was nearer if uninspiring.

There were birds to be seen from time to time, of course,
but what proved more surprising and more entertaining
than anything else were the mice. He hadn't expected to
see mice scurrying along the parapets and ledges of the
prison walls, their sharp little faces peering out of nooks
and crannies. A dozen times a day he clambered up on the
table to get a glimpse of them, or strain his ears to listen to
the exciting sound of motor bikes amidst the distant
rumble of traffic. Then he would jump down again, move
restlessly around, finger the books and magazines about
motor bikes he'd got from the prison library, sit down, lie
down, get up again, kick the slop bucket irritably, then
pick up the coarse canvas for making mail bags and start
stitching.

It gave him something to do, stitching those mail bags,
and though it was rough work, hard on his fingers, he took
a pride in what he had done. Even the warder commented
on the evenness of his stitches. He could do a good job
when he tried, as his teachers had realised when they wrote

on his school report, "This boy could do much better if he were to be less of a class comedian."

Now that he was alone for twenty-three out of every twenty-four hours, with no way of raising a laugh from an admiring audience, no one to incite to some wild escapade, nothing to do but get through the long period of solitary waiting for the pronouncement of judgment that he knew must go against him, he might as well do what he could to pass the time. Mealtimes made a welcome break in the monotony, hearing the warder unlocking his door, going out along the catwalk down to the kitchen, bringing his metal tray of food back to his cell, sitting down and eating it. After that there was nothing to look forward to till the next meal, or the half an hour's exercise walking round the courtyard twice a day.

Six weeks of that sort of life gave Vic plenty of time for a favourite indulgence – self-pity. He'd had a rough deal. Never known his parents; father died before he was two; mother deserted him and married again. The only time she ever did anything about him was to send a card on his eighth birthday with the words, "Love, Mum." That had upset him badly, because until that time he hadn't even known he'd got a "mum". Who was she, where was she and why didn't she ever come to see him? It would have been better not to have heard from her at all, rather than receive that one cryptic message out of the emptiness of his past.

It was shortly after that emotional disturbance that he had embarked on what had become his secret career as a thief. Not that he called himself a thief. It sounded too sneaky. He preferred the term "house-breaker", although that did not really describe him, either, since he did not break things up or leave a mess behind. As often as not he just walked in through an unlocked door, or crawled in at a window. In fact, he considered he behaved very decently, since when he found the money he was looking for he made it a rule only to take half, so as not to leave his victims in difficulties. No one seemed to give him any credit for that. And then a "shark" had split on him to the police! The fact that a number of his own victims had been people who had befriended and trusted him in no way lessened his sense of grievance. He sat on the hard mattress of the iron bedstead, moodily reviewing the past, gloomily looking into the future.

No hope for him there, he knew. His record was too bad – sent back to the orphanage after the couple who wanted to adopt him found his pockets full of stolen banknotes; dismissed from the Army Catering Corps for stealing Post Office savings books and forging signatures; six months at a probation hostel in Reading; then caught red-handed with the stolen camera, and deciding to ask for all his other burglaries to be taken into account as being the best way of getting clear of them. They made up to such a sizeable amount that he knew he couldn't avoid getting a prison sentence this time.

Oh, well! He'd get through it somehow. At any rate, it wouldn't be in solitary confinement like he was now, on remand. Once he was sentenced he'd be in with the other prisoners, there'd be the chance of getting up to a lark.

Vic was an optimist, and rarely cast down for long. He looked round now for some new way of passing the time. Those motor-biking books and magazines were depressing. When could he hope to feel again the throb of the machine between his knees, experience the thrill of power as he shot off down the road, swooped round the corner and, weaving in and out of the traffic, roared on to set the pace for the rest of the gang?

His eye caught the book on the ledge in the corner above his bed. He'd noticed it before, lying there in state, but seeing it was a New Testament he had ignored it.

"Might as well have a look at it," he thought, reaching his hand up. "Nothing better to do," and ignoring the preliminary pages he started reading Matthew's Gospel, doggedly wading through the long list of names, wondering what the word "begat" meant, then on to the narrative, which left him unimpressed, like reading a story that was in no way related to him. He jeered inwardly at the teaching about turning the other cheek, and being peacemakers. He'd seen what happened to the well-meaning blokes who tried to stop a fight in a bar. But he read on, dimly surprised, not at the miracles, which he'd heard about as a kid in the orphange, but at all those references to judgment.

The lawbreakers were going to be judged. The people who sneered at others were going to be judged. The people who didn't obey the teachings of Jesus were going to be judged. Those who blasphemed were going to be judged. Those stories Jesus told were about judgment too. The harvest, with the wheat gathered in, but the tares burnt. The servant who wouldn't forgive, and was thrown into prison. The indignant king judging those who had belittled his invitation to his son's wedding. Then a whole chapter about the Pharisees and their judgment. Another whole chapter about people who used their talents well, and those who didn't, those who helped others and those who didn't, all coming up for judgment.

Vic felt rather uneasy. Perhaps it was the relevance to his own immediate situation that made him note that theme of judgment. It seemed to run like a thread through the whole of Matthew's Gospel. Here he was, cooped up in a cell, waiting for the Winchester County Session when he would come up for trial, and judgment would be passed. And there was no way out.

He read on. The betrayal of Jesus, the trial, the crucifixion, the burial. It did not move him particularly, until he came to the last chapter, with the visit of the women to the tomb, the appearance of the angel and his words, "Do not be afraid; for I know that you seek Jesus who was crucified. He is not here; for He has risen, as He said. . ." followed a couple of verses later with the words, "And behold, Jesus met them . . ."

The reality of the resurrection of Jesus Christ hit Vic at last. Jesus had come to life again. He had said he would and he had. All that Jesus had said must be true, including what He had said about there being a judgment.

There in the cell that hot summer's day a sense of awe stole over Vic, and a sense of shame. He bowed his head.

What a wreck his life had been! There was no self-pity now. He was looking at the other side of the coin, not at what he had lacked but at what he had misused, not at the way people had failed him but at the way he had fooled them, with that open, ingenuous, cheerful face of his taking them in even while he was thieving from them. It was not so much the record of his eighteen years of life that stood out before him as the consciousness of what he was in himself – a despicable cheat.

What hope was there for a fellow like him? He was what he was, and he couldn't change himself. Like a drowning man wildly stretching out his hand to clutch at something that would save him from sinking, he flung himself down beside his bed, and in the only sort of language that came naturally to him he gasped out, "God, if you are there, you've got ten days to change my life, and if you haven't done it by then you've copped it."

If it sounded arrogant to the point of insolence, that was not the way he meant it. It was a cry for help. And the God who hears our cries, heard Vic that day.

Nothing spectacular happened. If Vic had expected some amazing revelation, some exalted feeling, he would have been disappointed, but he hadn't known what to expect. Instead, when he rose from his knees, he felt rather bewildered. A new dimension had opened up which he did not understand, and he had done something he'd never done before. He'd prayed to God.

He'd better tell someone. He'd got religion! He wondered if he was going round the bend. He went over to the corner of the cell and pulled the emergency bell.

*   *   *

On the face of it, Vic did not get much help from anyone when he tried to explain what had happened to him after he'd been reading in that Bible on the ledge in the cell. The warder who responded to the bell he rang so urgently was sceptical when he said he wanted to see the chaplain. The warder was used to prisoners wanting to see the chaplain – anything for a chat to relieve the monotony! Further explanation from Vic caused him to lift his eyebrows, shrug his shoulders and, after considering the merits of the case, to decide it was not in the Reverend Father's line, nor the Vicar's either. Better try the Nonconformist. So the following day the Nonconformist chaplain arrived and sat down beside Vic on the bed, rocking to and fro in a state of uncertainty as Vic told his story. He'd never heard anything like it before, he admitted, and did not know what to do. He was a kind man, kept an eye on Vic, and arranged for the *Methodist Recorder* to be delivered to him each week, but was unable to interpret the experience. Vic was left to work it out for himself, alone in his cell with that New Testament.

He did not get very far in his understanding, but got a long way in his desires, which underwent a most amazing change. He wanted to be a Christian, to be loved by God, to live a different sort of life, be a different sort of person, a clean, straight person. He wouldn't even mind not having a motor bike, if only he could live a clean straight life, like the followers of Jesus. He wondered what chance he would have, first serving his prison sentence, then going out into the world with that stigma on him, to look for a job. The future looked grey. "Help me, God!"

The cry again. God heard the cry.

As the time came up for his trial, a chain of circumstances was quietly set in motion. The probation officer appointed to deal with his case took his responsibilities seriously, prayed about the men he had to deal with, and decided this young fellow ought to have another chance. He put up such a moving appeal for him at the trial that the judge agreed not to send him to prison, but to put him on probation for three years, providing he spent the first one in an approved probation hostel. The warden there turned out to be a Christian, and challenged Vic to live like one. It took some courage on Vic's part, and self restraint too, but he managed to avoid being the first to go into a fight, even offering the other cheek when he was attacked. True, he made it plain that his Christian obligation ceased there, and anyone hitting his other cheek would get what was coming to him, but no one found fault with that.

He went along to church and there at last he learned what had happened to him. A talk with the pastor made it all clear. God has forgiven him all his sins that day in the cell when he cried out to Him. He had given him the gift of eternal life and was giving him the power to lead a new life.

"God is going to use you, my boy, you mark my words," said the hostel warden's wife encouragingly and, when a few weeks later he was baptised, six of the other hostel fellows, watching from the gallery, decided they wanted to become Christians too. They wanted what Vic had got. He was a gang leader again, but it was a different sort of gang.

Not everything went easily for him. Getting a job with his past record against him posed problems, his defective education posed others, and his unpredictable temperament even more. As he himself said, he didn't become a super-saint overnight. If it was a stiff climb, at any rate it was uphill, and the prophecy of the warden's wife came true.

He was a student at Spurgeon's Theological College, already marked out as one with an exceptional gift for evangelism,[1] when he went one day to Southampton to speak at a meeting. He was glad to be back in his home town where his record had been so bad, to tell of the change in his life, and how it had come about. The audience was enthusiastic, and plenty of people wanted to have a word with him when the meeting was over. Slowly he moved down towards the door as the crowd was thinning out, and looked smilingly at a man who came towards him rather diffidently. He looked as though he wanted to speak, and Vic stopped.

---

[1] Vic is now the executive vice-president of Evangelism Explosion International responsible for all Europe and Israel. He lives with his wife Sue and daughters Christy and Ruth in Southampton and attends the Grace Baptist Church which he founded in 1981. He has written two books, *Prison to Pulpit* and *A Hitch-hiker's Guide to Heaven*.

"I'm so glad to have heard you tonight," the man said. Then he added, "I'm the one who placed the Bibles in Winchester Prison just before you went in..."

Vic caught his breath. His mind flew back to that moment in the cell, twelve or more years ago now, when he had stretched up his hand to take down that book on the ledge over his bed. It had all started then. What would his life have been like if that little New Testament hadn't been there? And this was the man who had placed it!

For once, words failed Vic. He looked into the eyes of that Hampshire Gideon, and the Hampshire Gideon looked at him. There was silence for a moment, and then they did the only thing that seemed to give an adequate expression to their feelings. They flung their arms open and hugged each other.

7   Into the Swinging Sixties

Brother Fred did not limit himself to new-member dinners
as a means of recruiting for The Gideons. He enrolled
quite a number by personal persuasion among the
tradesmen with whom he was acquainted. Even if their
businesses were small they were their own masters, he
pointed out, and could arrange their affairs in such a way
as to be free to fulfil some Gideon duty, like visiting
someone whose name was sent from headquarters, or
arranging for a Bible placement somewhere. He expatiated
glowingly on the thrilling opportunities the organisation
presented to Christians in the business world. Head thrust
forward in his enthusiasm, he invariably won his man.

"Bang goes my new hat!" said the wife of one such
tradesman wryly as, standing behind the counter with
him, she watched him make out a cheque for the annual
subscription. Brother Fred grinned at her. In the long run
she'd get a crown instead of a hat, and one that wouldn't
wear out. He was never at a loss to strike the right note
when it came to repartee.

One of his friends owned a butcher's shop in Chiswick
and, when passing one day, Fred called in. Full of the
newly formed British branch of The Gideons, he could
talk of nothing else, and having told Arthur all about it
said: "You ought to join. It's just the thing for you.
Fellowship, inspiration, openings for you to preach the
Gospel you've never thought of. You ought to become a
Gideon."

So Arthur Rousham became a Gideon and when, a few
years later, he and his wife agreed that he should sell the
business and take an early retirement so that he could
spend all his time on matters of more permanent
importance than the making of more and more money, he

offered to give a day each week to help Brother Fred in the Gideon office.

There he began to experience for himself what Brother Fred had talked about. The Gideon office was the centre into which letters, phone calls, news, flowed from various sources. One never knew what would come next. There was the hotelier, for instance, who phoned asking for Bibles to be supplied to his establishment. Certainly! But just as a matter of interest, how did he know about The Gideons?

"Well, I've recently been released from prison, and while there I read the Bible I found in my cell. Now I've become a Christian. That's why I want a Bible in every room in my hotel. It may stop some man from crime." That particular request was responded to with even greater alacrity than usual. Arthur Rousham and Brother Fred were delighted to be reaching a stratum of life very different from the respectable, law-abiding church-goers to whom they were accustomed.

Then there was the experience related by the girl behind the counter of a draper's shop who excitedly spotted the little Gideon badge a customer was wearing and exclaimed,

"Oh, you're a Gideon!"

"Yes. Do you know them?"

"I ought to!" and she proceeded to tell her story.

She had taken a wrong step in life, and when her parents discovered how she was deceiving them, they turned her out of the house. How long it took for defiance to turn to despair she did not say, but she got to the point of deciding to commit suicide. She would fling herself in front of a train. But when she got to the railway line she could not pluck up courage to do it, nor into the water of the canal beside which she then walked. Then she remembered having read in a paper of someone who had thrown himself from a window. She would do it that way. She went to a hotel, booked the cheapest room they had, knowing it would be at the top, and went up to it. On entering she walked across to the window and leaned forward to open it, but a book on the ledge distracted her. Glancing down she saw that it was opened, and her eyes caught the words, "The wages of sin is death."

Death! Death was what she was wildly seeking, but the significance of its relation to sin had not struck her until now. To her distraught gaze the words seemed to be standing out in letters of fire. She tried to push the book away, but found she could not move. Some invisible power seemed to be gripping her and, struggle as she would, her efforts were unavailing. After a time she sank back, exhausted, and once more looking down at the book saw the words immediately following those that had so alarmed her: "But the gift of God is eternal life through Christ Jesus our Lord."

"I fell on my knees and cried to God for forgiveness, that He would give me this gift of eternal life. And after wrestling with myself for some time, peace came at last, and I knew that God had heard me. Though I cannot explain how, I knew my sins were forgiven, and that God's Word had saved me." She had gone home, told her parents of her experience, and they had welcomed her back into their hearts as well as their home. "How I thank God for that Bible in the hotel bedroom!"

In hospitals, too. One of the incidents related at The Gideons' office was of a woman who was dying of an incurable disease, and was burdened with apprehension at what lay before her. A nurse in the ward got in touch with a Baptist minister about her, but he was unable to go at the time. However, he had in his possession 800 Gideon New Testaments to be delivered in the hospital in four days' time, and taking one of them he handed it to the nurse. "Give this to her, and ask her to read it. I'll come to see her as soon as I can." When he arrived, a few days later, the woman greeted him with a smile. Holding up the New Testament she said, "I've found the way through reading this. I'm not afraid to die now."

Equally encouraging, if less spectacular, were the letters that came concerning the distribution of New Testaments to school children.

One young woman whose husband had deserted her after the birth of their child wrote of her depression and suicidal tendency, only resisted for the sake of her little girl. She had sought in vain for consolation, even starting to read the Bible but finding no relief. Then one day her little girl brought home a New Testament given to her by The Gideons.

"I began to read the Testament, and somehow it seemed different from the others. I began to find peace and help. I felt that someone cared for me, that the Lord Jesus had come to earth and died that I might have eternal life and peace with Him. And so it was through this that I received the Lord into my heart . . .'

Another mother, finding a New Testament with The Gideons' emblem under her son's pillow as she made his bed each day, had her curiosity aroused. What was it the child read so diligently before going to sleep? Day after day, in secret, she read it herself, and the result was that faith was born in her own heart. A father, after reading the New Testament his schoolgirl daughter had brought home, wrote to The Gideons' headquarters expressing his interest. Two local Gideons were put in touch with him, and the outcome was that both he and his wife became Christians.

Even more enlivening had been the visit to the office of a tall American business man, named Sam, once a criminal, who related his own story. He had landed up in hospital, seriously ill and, when a pastor came to see him, made it quite plain that he wanted nothing to do with religion, nor with the pastor either. So the pastor, unable to make any headway, turned to leave, but as he was doing so caught sight of the Gideon Bible on the locker. Picking it up he dropped it on the bed and said, "You'd better start reading this. You're not going to be here much longer." The effect was dramatic. Sam had not realised until then that he was dying.

"I started to read," he said, "and prayed for the first time in my life. God answered, and forgave me. Then the thought came to me – if God can save my soul, He can surely heal my body. And He did that, too... Do you wonder that I'm a Gideon myself now?" he added, pointing to his badge.

So it went on. It was not only when at the office that Arthur Rousham heard about the results of Gideon activity. He was away speaking at a Youth Fellowship on one occasion when the leader told him of a young sailor, known to him personally, who had been taken into hospital after a drunken brawl, had seen the Gideon Testament on his locker, and had been converted through reading it. And he gladly took second place as a speaker at a meeting in Norwich, when an AA scout spoke for twenty minutes on how, when he was at the point of suicide through personal difficulties, he had come across his son's Gideon New Testament when sorting through a drawer, had started reading it, and his life had been revolutionised.

Not that all were success stories. Arthur, like others, had his disappointments. A letter from the Waldorf Hotel was followed up by the arrival in the office of a young man who asked for a Bible like the one in his room at the hotel. Further conversation elicited the information that he was a guardsman, that his parents were in the Salvation Army, and that he himself was at last prepared to ask God to come into his life. Arthur's heart was warmed as they knelt in prayer together and, as they rose from their knees, the young man promised to keep in touch. That was the last Arthur ever saw or heard of him.

Even more discouraging was the case of the prisoner who had written from Dartmoor professing conversion, who turned up at the office after his release with a very convincing story of what reading the Bible in his cell had meant to him. Well dressed, well spoken, he made a good impression, especially when he made it quite plain that he did not want money. He was an accountant, and what he wanted was a job. He did not try to hide the fact that he'd done seven years for embezzlement, due to gambling. Now he wanted to make good.

Arthur phoned a Gideon who was an accountant and received the answer, "We've got a vacancy right now. Send him along to see me." He went, and was given the job.

"How's he getting on?" enquired Arthur some time later.

"Well, we've got one or two doubts," was the rather reluctant answer. Then, a few weeks later, "He's been leaving the office at odd times... found he was going to the bookmakers..." Finally, "We've had to get rid of him."

Arthur knew his Bible too well to be disillusioned, and so did Brother Fred, who had had similar experiences. Had not the Lord Himself said that seed was sown with varying results, that some blossomed quickly and then withered, some got choked with weeds, and that some never really took root at all? But He had also said that some fell into good ground and produced a good harvest. What was certain was that if much seed were sown there would be a rich harvest, if little seed were sown there would be a poor one, and if no seed were sown there would be no harvest at all. So it was with undiminished enthusiasm that they entered the next phase of Gideon work in Britain.

* * *

It has been claimed that the permissive element in British social life was ushered in with the famous case in the Old Bailey over D.H. Lawrence's book *Lady Chatterley's Lover*, in 1960. Until that time the book had been banned by the censor. An enterprising publishing firm courted prosecution by producing an edition of the novel, and the case came up for trial. When the jury of twelve members of the public, having duly perused it, proclaimed in favour of the publishers, censorship was forced to take a broader view, conforming with the general "live and let live" attitude towards morality that characterised the Swinging Sixties. It marked the beginning of a new era in which easy divorce, "one-parent families", sexual perversion and other ills of a sick society were to become increasingly evident. If the rot had already set in, the decade that started in 1960 revealed it.

Morally destructive forces were being unleashed, but

they were not to go unchallenged. If the full story of that decade were to be told it would include the mobilising of several new units in what might be termed the army of resistance to those malign agencies. As far as The Gideons were concerned, mobilisation had commenced ten years before, but the beginning of the 1960s saw a fresh advance with the formation of its Development Committee.

The purpose of the Development Committee, as its name implies, was to expand the activities of The Gideons, and they set about it in a practical, down-to-earth way. "This is a job of work," said Norman Wyatt, its chairman. "And business men whose training has been in selling and servicing are the ones to do it." They gathered in The Gideons' office, where a map on the wall indicated the location of existing Gideon local branches. They studied the map carefully, and laid their plans. Brother Fred, fervent as ever, was brimming over with the idea.

"This is the first time since the formation of The Gideons in this country that I have ever heard discussed serious plans to put the work on to a truly national basis," he exclaimed, and gave them his earnest attention. Those vast areas on the map of the British Isles in which there was not a dot to indicate that a local branch existed – something must be done about them! The placing of Bibles in every hotel during the Coronation Year had been a magnificent effort, but the effect was short-lived. What was needed now was groups of Christian business men throughout the country who would maintain and expand the enterprise of placing Bibles in the traffic lanes of their own communities – the schools, the hospitals, the prisons as well as the hotels. Gideon branches must be established all over the country.

So the Development Committee got down to work. The help of Christian business and professional men in strategic areas was enlisted, visits paid to ministers, contacts made. Slowly but steadily new branches were formed. The influence of The Gideons was widening.

It all kept Brother Fred busier than ever, while Arthur Rousham found there was scarcely time to swallow his sandwiches on the day each week he spent in The Gideons' office. There was nothing he did not know about what was going on, and he felt there was no emergency that could take him entirely by surprise after he'd interviewed some of the visitors who arrived unannounced, including ex-prisoners who came along with their problems. It all proved a good preparation for the telephone call that reached him at home one day, although it came as a surprise at the time. It was from the head typist in The Gideons' office.

"Mr. Rousham, can you come up. Mr. Bradbury's been suddenly taken into hospital for an operation. We can't cope on our own, especially with the visitors. Can you come. . . ?"

He went, of course, ready to fill the gap for as long as was needed. It proved to be longer than he had anticipated. If he had any doubts as to whether he was employing his time in the right way, they were dispelled by the significant timing of two apparently unrelated incidents. The first occurred when he was driving home from a Gideon assignment. He had been thinking about this new way that seemed to be opening up before him, and longed for a confirmation that it was the right one. As he drove along the motorway on that showery day, there appeared before him the colourful phenomenon of a rainbow. There was nothing particularly unusual about that, but it was distinctive in that it was an unbroken arc which straddled the road before him, and it seemed like a reassuring omen. A very short time afterwards, the favourable sale of a property he owned released all the money he needed to continue working for The Gideons. Everything was fitting into place.

Brother Fred was out of action for some time, and although he made a good recovery eventually, it was evident that he could not again shoulder the responsibilities as well as the activities of general secretary. Arthur Rousham was the man for that now, and there were other ways in which Brother Fred's enthusiasm and experience could be used. Even while he was in hospital he had been visited by Leonard Crimp, vice-president of Heinz, who was on his way to India to see about starting Gideon work there. He had found the patient eager to hear his news and, when he told him all about his plans, Brother Fred had said earnestly, "I'll pray for you, Len," and he had been as good as his word. He'd got a map of India, marked the places where Len was going, followed him in thought and prayer, became excited about the new branches that had eventually been established. The International Cabinet, very fond of Brother Fred, and knowing he'd been somewhat disappointed during the years of the constitutional crisis by the decision to keep all overseas work in its own hands, had an idea. Now that he was on his feet again, why not ask him to go to India himself, to encourage, to inspire, to instruct and generally enthuse some of the branches that had been established there?

He had a great time in India, although he set off with some apprehensions, never having been there before, wondering how he'd get on in the hot climate, and hoping that everyone he met would speak English. When he arrived it took him four hours to get through Customs at Madras, but after that things went smoothly.

He was greeted by the local Gideon president and his wife, whisked off to a hotel, and plunged immediately into a whirl of Gideon activity. Visits to schools where the principals, fearful of giving offence to rigid religionists, tried to restrict the presentation of Bibles to children of the Christian caste but had to give way to the vociferous demands of Hindu pupils who wanted them too. Visits to hospitals where dark-skinned nurses queued up to receive the New Testaments being handed to them. Visits to hotels, one of them owned by a Muslim who attended the ceremony which always accompanies Bible presentations, and where a couple of American business men staying in the place also expressed their gratification at being present. They'd travelled widely and had appreciated the Gideon Bibles they'd found in their hotel rooms, but they'd never seen The Gideons themselves in action before. And, of course, there were some New Member

Banquets arranged, at which Mr. F.W. Bradbury, the national secretary of The Gideons, out from England on a special visit, was the guest speaker.

He went on to Ceylon from India, and altogether had a very successful and profitable time. Neither he nor anyone else could have known that the most important outcome of his visit was to be not so much the influence on the Indian branches but on the Scotsman who, because he was a missionary, could not be enrolled as a Gideon.

8 Missionary Turns Gideon

Ian Hall was born in India, his father being in the Indian Forest Service, and, having picked up Hindi as a child, he was as much at home in that country as in Britain. He had served in the Indian Army during the Second World War, and, after qualifying as a printer, had gone back to join the team of Brethren missionaries, working first in Bombay and latterly in Bangalore. He was well established as the business manager of Clarence High School by 1962, when Brother Fred arrived with his enthusiastic introduction to The Gideons, and there he would probably have remained had it not been for his family responsibilities.

The three boys were in their teens by now, and he and Rita were already wondering if their duty lay in making a home for them in Britain, where their education could be completed, when Rita developed a serious kidney complaint. This settled the matter. She could not remain in India if she was to survive, the doctors said. So, as they were due for leave anyway, they returned to Scotland, and in between the deputation meetings at which he had been booked to speak for the first few months, Ian set about looking for a job.

Meanwhile, unknown to him, The Gideons were looking for another member of staff. It was while he was in Southport, where he had speaking engagements, that he heard about it. He was staying with The Gideons' national chaplain, John Dalgleish, who said to him, "The Gideon work in this country is growing. Rousham's got more than enough to do with all the letters and phone calls he gets in the office. He can't take advantage of all the opportunities there are to get new branches going, and encourage those already established. We're going to advertise for someone to do the field work. Why don't you apply?"

"But am I eligible – a missionary?"

"You're a missionary on leave now, but you won't be much longer. You'll be back in the secular world, looking for a job! And the work you were doing was a business job, anyway, whatever preaching and teaching you may have done in your spare time. Think about it – pray about it. I'll pray too."

On the face of it the job seemed tailor-made for him, but as he talked it over with Rita they both realised there was one drawback. The salary The Gideons would be offering was far below that being offered by Horlicks, who were wanting an area sales manager, and Ian, who had applied for the job, had already been short-listed. Without a home of their own, and with three boys still at school, they felt they needed the money, and it was in a state of some uncertainty that they went to a service one Sunday morning when the word "counterfeit", repeated several times in the sermon, arrested their attention. The preacher spoke about counterfeit money, counterfeit Christians and counterfeit pleasures.

Conscious of the young people in his congregation who were contemplating launching out on their careers, the preacher continued: "And there are counterfeit jobs. There are the jobs that offer high salaries and good prospects and plenty of perks – but no fulfilment..."

Ian and Rita instinctively glanced at each other, and their eyes met with complete understanding as the preacher was saying, "You could be missing the very job God has for you – the job He's prepared for you – the job He wants you to do. The job in which you will find fulfilment."

It was quite unnecessary for them to say much as they talked it over later. They had got the message. They could manage on a smaller salary, they agreed, and anyhow, "... seek first His kingdom and His righteousness, and all these things shall be yours as well". They had proved the promise true in the past, they'd trust it for the future.

Ian applied for the Gideon job and when he was interviewed the Council decided that, of the men they were considering, he was the one they wanted. He joined the staff as field secretary in June 1965, and soon discovered that there were problems demanding wisdom, as well as opportunities calling for enterprise, within the movement. The constitutional crisis was over, and the rulings of the International Cabinet were accepted, but now another spirited debate was in progress. In what version should the Bible and New Testaments for Great Britain be printed?

At the beginning of the work in 1950 there had been no question about it. The Gideons distributed their Bibles and New Testaments in the King James (Authorised) Version. Now, however, there was an increasing demand, especially from schools, for the more modern versions. One headmaster, typical of many, wrote:

> I thank you for your very generous offer, but in fact we now use the New English Bible, and have a large number of AV New Testaments for which we now have no use. It has taken me a decade of teaching the Bible to believe that children today cannot understand the AV. I used to think they just *would* not and used to nag away and say I had no difficulty at this age, etc. Whether the language has moved decisively further from 17th century English in my lifetime, or whether they lack patience, or what the cause is...

The fact evidently remained that the AV editions were no longer very acceptable in schools. The same criticism came from many of the branches regarding the Bibles distributed in hospitals and other institutions. "The thees and the thous, the couldests and the doeths – people simply can't cope with them. People aren't used to old English. We ought to be using a modern version."

If some of the diehards among the British Gideons themselves were strongly opposed to any change, the International Council, surprisingly enough, was even more so. As Ian travelled throughout the British Isles visiting Gideon branches the subject was one which continually recurred, while Norman Wyatt's three-year term of office as president from 1963 to 1966 was heavily punctuated with correspondence on the subject. The International Cabinet wisely insisted that there should be uniformity in The Gideons' distribution of Bibles in English, and until convinced of the rightness of adopting one of the modern versions, was sticking to the safe and well-tried AV. By the end of 1966 the debate was still continuing. In a letter addressed to the international director, the increasing urgency of the matter was pressed:

> ... it would be only right and proper for the International Cabinet to find out from all the English-speaking branches and national associations how much they need a modern version. If we in England find this important, and our friends in Australia similarly, I can imagine the issue is even more urgent in the countries of the Caribbean, in Africa, in India where English is the first international language but not the native language of the people. You may remember that great order from Ghana about 18 months ago to the British and Foreign Bible Society for 500,000 copies of the Bible, an order which has now been completed. At first 80,000 copies of the King James Version were forwarded but immediately on receipt of these they requested that all other copies of the Scriptures be in a modern version ...

Over the next few years the question of a suitable modern version was a "hot" item on the agenda of successive annual general meetings while the National Council quietly and thoroughly investigated the theological soundness and reliability of the many modern versions which were available. After much discussion it seemed that none of the existing modern versions would have the unanimous support of either the British Isles membership or the International Cabinet.

Then, out of the blue, came a suggestion from Dr. Donald Guthrie, one of the foremost New Testament Greek scholars in the British Isles and a lecturer at the

London Bible College, that The Gideons might consider a
new translation which was shortly to be published. It was
called the ACT – A Contemporary Translation – and the
work was being carried out by a panel of one hundred
international scholars who were all conservative evangeli-
cals.

The theological pedigree of this new translation
sounded good but there were a few major problems. Could
the National Council confidently commit itself to a new
translation that hadn't yet had time to prove its worth on
the commercial market and run the risk of it being dubbed
a Gideon translation? And would the International
Cabinet approve a version, however theologically sound,
before it had had time to prove its acceptability by the
main stream churches?

The British Isles national president during this crucial
period was Douglas Fearn, the registrar of county courts at
Kingston, and he and Ian Hall spent many hours together
researching this new translation and helping to produce
an anglicised edition of what eventually became known as
the New International Version (NIV). They also made
several trips across the Atlantic to discuss the project with
the International Cabinet.

The breakthrough came when Ian Hall was invited to
address the International Cabinet at its meeting in
Albuquerque, New Mexico in February 1973. The Cabinet
generously allowed five hours for Ian Hall to present his
case and for the discussion which followed. When the
meeting was over, one Cabinet member shook Ian's hand
warmly and said, "Well, dear brother, you were so well
briefed that your case was won before you ever stepped into
the room!"

In April 1974 the New Testament in the New
International Version was made available to the British
Isles Gideons "as an alternative to the Authorised Version,
where requested." By the end of its first year of use over
fifty per cent of Youth Testament distribution was in this
version and it wasn't long before over ninety per cent of
school distribution was in the NIV. If the National

Council had any doubts as to its acceptability, these doubts were rapidly dispelled by the greatly increased volume of letters of testimony from both pupils and teachers, commenting appreciatively on its readability and reliability. Today, all Gideon Scriptures, with the exception of large-type editions for use by the elderly, are available in the NIV.

For Ian, in his field work, there was the task of initiating Gideons into the somewhat delicate art of approaching hotel managers, school principals, prison governors and the like with the offer of Scriptures, and later, of behaviour at the presentation. Arthur Rousham had produced a number of guidelines on this subject, ranging from hints on appearance – "Remember you stand as a Christian business or professional man. Look the part. This is not the time for a sports coat and flannel trousers..." – to a hypothetical interview with a reluctant hotel manager who was won over by the courteous and practical persuasion of the Gideon.

"But make it plain that there must be no high-pressure salesmanship in order to place Bibles," he warned. "In the last few years a considerable number of unused hotel Bibles have been returned to HQ because they were never really wanted in the first place... This is not good stewardship. Tell them not to pull strings or try to get in the back door. If the manager says 'No' it is all wrong to write to the owners." Harm had sometimes been done by well-meaning but over-zealous Gideons. Much better to enter the fray well prepared with a copy of a hotel Bible, along with a list of well-known hotels that had already received Bibles – the London Hilton, for instance, Carlton Towers, Trust House Hotels in Sheffield... "If they're good enough for the Hilton they're good enough for me," the manager would probably think. And, of course, the most important preparation would only be seen by God. Arthur Rousham never failed to refer to the activity which, as a Gideon, he might have felt would be taken for granted. "We can go further on our knees than any other way," as Dr. Graham Scroggie used to say.

Armed with hints and practical advice for the Gideon branches he was asked to visit, Ian had taken to the road, while Rita settled into the little house in Brentwood unexpectedly made available to them through the generosity of a Christian trust, and made it home.

They never had the slightest doubt that the decision to turn down the job in Horlicks (which was offered to Ian) was the right one. It had been said: "Satan can deceive by counterfeit guidance, but there is one thing he cannot imitate – that is the deep peace of God in the heart when we are in line with His will." They knew it to be true. There was the fulfilment that had been referred to as well. It was exciting to be at the receiving end of the sort of stories Fred Bradbury had told so vividly at that dinner in Bangalore. One such story appeared first, not in a letter to The Gideons' office, but in an issue of the *Sunday Post* under the title, "Message that Saved a Glasgow Woman's Life". The story ran:

Not long ago, a woman locked the door of a Glasgow hotel room behind her, and closed the window tightly.

Then, without putting a match to the gas fire, she turned it on and lay down on the bed. Lonely, desolate and afraid of the future, she had made up her mind to end it all. But as she lay listening to the hiss of the escaping gas her eyes fell on a book on the bedside table. She picked it up and opened it. It was a Bible – and as she read, she suddenly realised the awful thing she was doing to herself. For her eyes lit on these words – "Ye are not your own, ye are bought with a price."

She realised, too, that it wasn't too late to begin again – so she rose from the bed, threw open the window and turned off the gas. Then, like a new woman, she went out into the life she had so nearly lost for ever . . .

It was a Gideon Bible that gave the Glasgow woman the will to live again, and I know she is only one of countless hundreds who could tell the same story.

Very seldom was Gideon work written up in a large

circulation newspaper, so it was even more surprising to find a leader in the same issue referring to it, and taking up the cudgels for The Gideons by demanding to know why the British Railways Board still continued to refuse to have Gideon Bibles placed in their hotels.

Perhaps the highlight of Ian's early years on The Gideons' staff, however, was the letter that reached the office from a hotel in Russell Square. It was written by an Indian staying there, who said he had read the suggested readings for "Where to Find Help when Afraid and Anxious" in the Bible by his bed, and would like to know more.

Ian promptly went round to the hotel, explained to the receptionist that he had come from The Gideons in response to a letter from a guest, and was invited up to a room on the first floor. There he was greeted courteously by a well-dressed elderly Indian whose eyes opened wide with surprise when Ian responded in perfect Hindi.

"You speak my language?" the man exclaimed. After that, conversation was easy, and the man briefly told his story. He had come to England for specialist surgery. He had been diagnosed as having a tumour on the brain, and was to have an operation. That was why, as a result of what he had read in the holy book so unexpectedly found in his room, he had written to ask for further spiritual enlightenment. He was very grateful that his request had met with so ready a response, for he was to go into hospital the next day. He had been told there was only a fifty-fifty chance of the operation being successful.

The dark eyes looked into Ian's, intelligent, questing eyes, the eyes of a man facing death, and Ian nodded silently, and reached out his hand for the Bible . . .

*　　*　　*

"I never had such an opportunity all the time I was in India," he told Rita that evening on his return home. "The man was ready to listen, to give his whole attention to what I had to tell him – that Jesus Christ, God's only

Son, died and came to life again, and that He holds the keys of death and of the unseen world...

"And to think that if I'd been in India I would never have met him at all. What likelihood of an insignificant missionary having a heart-to-heart talk with an important member of the Indian government, ending up with prayer together, in the Name of Jesus!"

"Who was he?" Rita asked.

"Mr. G.G. Swell, the deputy speaker of the Lok Sabbha, India's parliament."

9   Message from the Moon

Scientifically speaking, the highlight of the year 1968 was the first manned space flight round the moon. The attention of the world was focussed on Apollo Eight as it circumnavigated the pale globe whose reflected light preserved Earth from almost total darkness during the hours of night. The moon! Queen of the night, that mysterious body in the heavens that had stirred the imagination and emotions of mankind since the beginning of time! And now man had actually reached it, by-passed it, was emerging from behind it, and intricately-designed, powerful machines were relaying the sights and the sounds from the tiny spacecraft spinning through outer space at an incredible rate, hundreds of thousands of miles away.

Literally millions of people the world over had their eyes glued to their TV sets and their ears cocked for the running commentary coming over the air that Christmas Eve. It was maximum viewing time, and then the commander of the little three-man team announced: "We are now approaching lunar sunrise, and for all the people back on Earth the crew of Apollo Eight has a message we would like to send you."

The listening world, as it were, held its breath. What would it be, that first message from the moon? Then Commander Borman's voice continued, on a slightly different note, as of one reading out an important communiqué:

In the beginning God created the heaven and the earth. And the earth was without form, and void; and darkness was upon the face of the deep.

And the Spirit of God moved on the face of the waters.

And God said, Let there be light: and there was light.
And God saw the light that it was good:
And God divided the light from the darkness ...

The newsmen waiting eagerly for every word that came from the spacecraft were taken aback. The reaction of the first men to come so close to the moon, making scientific history as they were, was important, and here they were focussing attention, not on what they could see, but on what they could not see – "In the beginning, God ..." Some comment was called for, and the NBC – TV science editor announced in a rather bewildered voice, "The men have just read from the Bible." He had not been expecting it, that was evident. "If memory from my youth serves me correctly," he continued, "it is from the book of Genesis."

His memory was serving him correctly. The reading was from Genesis, one of the best-known passages in the Bible, but never before in the history of mankind had so many millions heard at one time those words that so unequivocally pronounce the fact of a Creator. Coming from the lips of men who were in the forefront of scientific discovery, the stark simplicity of those words was the more solemnising.

Not everyone who heard them recognised them, of course. One of the many telephone calls received at NASA's newsroom in Houston, Texas, was from a Japanese newsman, who asked if someone would read him a transcript of the message. He had been unable to get it.

"Where are you?" asked the public affairs officer.

"In my hotel room," was the reply.

"Well, look in your bureau, and you'll see a book called the Holy Bible," said the officer. "You'll find what they said at the beginning of the very first chapter."

The Japanese newsman was considerably impressed by the efficiency of NASA's public relations office. To find the exact transcript of what had been said from the moon right there in his hotel bedroom! He did not realise at the time that the public relations office could not claim all the credit, for the Bible in the bedroom had been placed there by The Gideons.

So had the Bible on board Apollo Eight.

This is how it had come about.

An enterprising Gideon, realising that there was the potential for a branch in Pasadena, arranged for a New Member Dinner to be held there in August 1968, and one of those who attended and enrolled as a Gideon was the chief of the Flight Technical Branch of the Manned Spacecraft Centre. He attended the regular meetings held by the newly-formed Gideon branch, and in November one of the members referred to the imminent launching of Apollo Eight. Should they not pray that copies of God's Word could be placed on the spacecraft? As they were praying, the chief had an idea. There might be something he could do about this. So he got in touch with the public affairs office at the centre, and eventually reached Commander Borman by telephone.

"Have you got a copy of the Bible on Apollo Eight?" he asked.

"No," was the reply.

This was the moment to introduce the work of The Gideons, of whom Commander Borman apparently already knew something, having come across the Bibles they had placed in hotels and motels where he had stayed. Would he be willing for the crew of Apollo Eight to receive copies for the spacecraft? Yes, he would be delighted. So the presentation was duly made, Apollo Eight set off on its flight to the moon, and Gideons in Pasadena prayed earnestly that somehow or other something from the Word of God would come from space.

When it happened, it proved to be even more significant and impressive than they had hoped. As the chief of the Flight Technical Branch of the Manned Spacecraft Centre in Pasadena listened to it he was so overjoyed that, to quote his own words, he nearly went through the ceiling.

Meanwhile, in Great Britain preparations were being made for the launching of another vessel, one of a more conventional type, but not without its claim to inter-national interest. The Cunard luxury liner, *Queen Elizabeth II* was nearing completion, the docks at Liverpool were alive with workmen, final touches were

being put to the sumptuous lounges and elegant
staterooms, and applications were pouring in for the
privilege of being passengers on its maiden voyage.
Altogether, the *QE II* was in the news and the attention of
The Gideons was arrested.

Their job was to place Bibles within the reach of those
in the traffic lanes of life – visitors in hotels, children
changing schools, patients in hospital, law-breakers in
prison. They were all people in transit – and did not
people in transit also include passengers on luxury liners?
Their economic situation and social status might put
them in a more exclusive line of traffic from most of the
others, but their basic spiritual needs were no different. At
the end of the journey of life they'd find themselves at
exactly the same point as everyone else. And if they
hadn't got things straightened out by then, they'd find the
very economic and social assets with which they had sailed
through life suddenly turning up on the debit side of their
account as having been squandered on themselves rather
than used for the benefit of others.

In any case, travellers on luxury liners were no more
immune from the griefs and the failures, the disappointments and the temptations of everyday existence than were
others, and in the Bible could be found the remedy they all
needed. The Gideons agreed that those who travelled on
the *QE II* ought to have the Book, so when a courteously
worded letter was received at headquarters on Cunard-
headed notepaper, actually asking if 1,000 Gideon Bibles
could be supplied for the liner, it might have been
expected to evoke nothing but delight, especially as the
timing of events was so propitious. Scripture distribution
through The Gideons in the British Isles was approaching
the four-million mark – what better way of commemorating the occasion than by presenting the captain
of the *QE II* with the four-millionth copy at the ceremony
when the 1,000 Bibles that had been requested were
delivered?

The prospect was picturesque and would have been
exciting were it not for one drawback which put a curb on

Ian Hall's enthusiasm. It was not that there was likely to be any difficulty in arranging for the presentation – Cunard themselves had asked for it. It was not that the printers would not be able to execute the order in time. Collins had always proved most cooperative in such matters.

No, the drawback was of another nature, centred entirely in the treasury of the British Isles Gideons. In a word, The Gideons were hard up. There was no money in the kitty. And this time they knew they could not look for help from across the Atlantic. The American Gideons were steadily reducing their financial aid, according to the plan already agreed on by both sides, for the aim was the same – that the British Gideons should be self-supporting.

The plan was a good one, but the implementation of it was not without difficulty. The annual subscriptions paid by The Gideons covered all the costs of administration, so money given for Bibles was used exclusively for that purpose. However, comparatively little money was being donated from outside sources for Bibles in "the swinging sixties". The Gideons in the various branches, eager to grasp every opportunity they saw of placing Bibles, dipped into their own pockets to pay for them, and such donations as were received at headquarters were rapidly swallowed up in response to letters from the branches telling of wonderful openings, and asking for grants to help buy all the Bibles and Testaments required. In fact, when the request from Cunard came, Ian had just written to all the branches explaining that they'd better go slow on arranging for Scripture distribution unless they themselves could foot the bills, since Gideon funds were at an all-time low.

On the face of it, therefore, the possibility of supplying 1,000 handsomely-bound Bibles suitable for display in the *QE II*'s luxury cabins, was rather remote. Yet somehow, Ian was stimulated, not disheartened. It was the custom for the staff in the office to spend twenty minutes in prayer each day before starting work, so on that April morning in 1968 he read the letter from Cunard out to them, and said it was a challenge to their faith. The Gideon coffers were empty – would God, in answer to their prayers, supply the money that was needed?

The prayer meeting that morning was more than usually urgent, for a reply must be sent to Cunard within the next few days, and an order for the Bibles lodged if the request were to be met. "Oh, Lord! The silver and the gold are Yours... We pray that You will send the money we need for those Bibles for Cunard – soon..."

Then everyone dispersed and got on with their various jobs, and Ian got on with his. There were letters to be answered and meetings to be prepared for – that one in Harlow in a couple of days time was the next on the list, when he was due to speak at a rally organised by the North-East London branch for "Friends of The Gideons". He went through his files to see what recent news had come in.

He thought of the case of the Indian doctor of the Brahmin caste, who had come to England for further studies, and whose first contact with live Christianity was at an evening party in Bristol, where a young nurse, the only one besides himself drinking orange juice instead of alcohol, explained that she was a Christian, and advised him to read the Bible if he wanted to find the truth about life. There was something about the girl's sincerity and quiet assurance that impressed him, and back in his room he found a copy of the very book she had spoken about. It was a Bible placed by The Gideons, and as he read it he was immediately struck by its note of authority. He went on reading... The full story of his journey into faith in Christ, his rejection by his family who had him placed in a mental hospital as being out of his mind, his deliverance and his upward climb in his profession would be all too long to tell, but what can be told is that Dr. Nambudripad was becoming one of the foremost neuro-surgeons in India – and one of its most ardent Gideons as well. He had good reason to believe in placing Bibles in hotel bedrooms.

Then there was the case of the young woman who, to

quote her own words, had dwelt "in the heart of rebel youthland – Chelsea." But the more boyfriends and late nights she had, and the more lies she told her parents, the unhappier she became. Then she fell in love, and everything was transformed until suddenly her dreams of marriage were shattered, and she found herself despairing, not knowing where to turn for help.

At that point the little Gideon Nurse Testament, that had been given to her long before, came to her aid. She looked up the verses under *Temptation* then those under *Failure*, and unexpectedly hope was given as she read: "There hath no temptation taken you but such as is common to man: but God is faithful, who will not suffer you to be tempted above that ye are able; but will with the temptation also make a way to escape, that ye may be able to bear it."

"So I claimed these promises for myself, asking to be delivered from my plight," she related later. "I made a bargain with God, that if He, through His Son Jesus Christ, could get me back on the right path, then He could have my life. . ."

It was good to be able to report that she had not only got back on to the right road, delivered from her plight, but was now a missionary, Ian reflected. These "Friends of The Gideons", who did so much to support the work, though not themselves Gideons, deserved to hear some of the things that happened through the Scriptures they supplied. It was encouraging to be able to tell them of continuing opportunities to distribute them, too, so he went to the meeting at Harlow and mentioned the request for Bibles for the *QE II*. He did not say that there was no money in hand to supply them, or how much they would cost, so it was rather surprising that a telephone call to the office next day should be to enquire, "How much would it cost to provide those Bibles for the *QE II*?"

Ian made a quick mental miscalculation when he answered "about £350", for he realised after putting down the receiver that the cost would be nearer £400. Too late to do anything about it now, he decided – anyway, he thought, it was only a casual enquiry. But it was not a casual enquiry. Two days later a cheque arrived for Bibles for the *QE II*, and to ensure that it covered the whole cost of the presentation, the donors had made it out for £400.

Some weeks later a little group of Gideons and friends went aboard the liner for the official presentation of the Bibles. It was preceded by a personally conducted tour of the vessel, led by Cunard's assistant managing director, and followed by a visit to the bridge. The spaciousness and elegance of the tourist accommodation, the dignified luxury of the de luxe cabins, the beauty of the Queen's Room – it all made them catch their breath, and they thought of the millionaires and the celebrities, the brave and the beautiful who would be travelling on this floating palace in years to come. The highlight of that memorable visit, however, was the half hour spent in the captain's private suite, when the presentation, including the four-millionth Bible as a personal gift to him, was made.

Ian, as national secretary of The Gideons, read Psalm 107, the mariner's psalm. The national vice-president offered the dedicatory prayer. The national president spoke about the work of The Gideons, and made the actual presentation. The genial captain of the *QE II* thanked The Gideons warmly for the gift.

And a retired police officer with his wife stood quietly in the group, looking with satisfaction at the 1,000 elegantly bound Bibles with their Gideon emblem stacked in a well-balanced display, ready to be placed, after the simple ceremony, in all the cabins throughout the ship. Harry and Betty Shorthouse had been at the meeting in Harlow for "Friends of The Gideons", and when they had got home that night they had had a little discussion as to how they would spend the legacy they had recently received. They had already decided to use it either to buy a car, or to take the trip of a lifetime to the Holy Land, but now they had changed their minds. A better way of using the money had presented itself. They would pay for that placement of Bibles on the *QE II* instead.

Theirs had been the phone call enquiring how much

money would be needed. Theirs had been the cheque for £400 to cover the entire cost. And theirs were the significant smiles as, from time to time over the years that followed, they heard of the need for replacements on the *QE II*, as one or another of the millionaires and the celebrities, the brave and the beautiful had evidently so much appreciated the Bibles they had found in their cabins that they had quietly walked off with them. The retired police officer was prepared to turn a very indulgent blind eye on that sort of petty pilfering. He was glad to know that the Bibles as well as the people were in transit. One never knew when the living messages the Book contained would find a receptive heart, or where it would be deposited in the course of its travels.

The coloured boy in South Africa who found one on the beach at Cape Peninsula after a fire in a hotel little knew what he had come across. He just saw a nicely bound book among the charred remains of furniture that had been thrown out, and picking it up slipped it inside his ragged jacket and made for home, several miles away on the other side of Table Mountain. Once there he cleaned it up and others in the village came to look at it. They were so interested that they started reading it together, with the introductory notes to guide them. When missionaries arrived on the scene, some time later, they found a group of people already prepared for the message they had to bring.

"Soon a little church was built," reported an official of Girls Brigade International who visited the place, "and the precious Bible which had meant so much in bringing them to faith in Christ was given a place of honour on a small improvised pulpit – thumbed and worn, with its hard-backed cover showing signs of fire and sea water." That Bible's journey started in the bedroom of a comfortable hotel, but it reached its place of true usefulness via the rubbish heap.

Bibles in hotel bedrooms that go missing, for one reason or another, sometimes turn up in apparently inaccessible places, as a *Daily Telegraph* news item reported on one occasion. Ten British mercenaries, imprisoned in Angola, cooped up in tiny cells, would have been beyond the reach of the most enterprising Gideon distributor, but all the same a Bible found its way into their cell. The advocate of one of the men, who had travelled out from Edinburgh to represent him when he came up for trial, had access to him and saw his need of something to occupy his mind in the dreary time of waiting. He wondered what he could do to help him, when his eye fell on something which gave him an idea: "I have just taken the Gideon Bible from my hotel room and given it to Cecil Fortiun..."

The Gideons who happened to see that news item were encouraged to go on praying for Bibles in transit. It is doubtful, however, whether they got quite so excited as did those who were gathered at an international convention in Chicago and heard a speaker from a turbulent South American country tell the following story:

> Ten years ago fifty men were detained in a military camp. They were charged with trying to overthrow the government of the country, and were sentenced by the revolutionary court to be shot.
>
> Three days before the sentence was to be carried out, a Gideon New Testament was dropped into their cell. For the next three days and nights the prisoners spent their time praying and reading the Scriptures. The morning came when they were to be killed. They continued to pray. They asked Jesus to take over their lives...
>
> Inexplicably the execution was postponed. Three months later the men were set free and the government apologised.

The speaker paused, then said in a voice charged with emotion:

> I want you to know that I was one of those men, now I am a Gideon!

10   Personally Speaking

The chief claim to distinction of the small market town of Lutterworth in Leicestershire is that John Wycliffe, morning star of the Reformation, the first translator of the Bible into the English language, lived and died there. Its chief claim to convenience, as Ian Hall saw it, was its proximity to the junction of the M1 and M6 motorways. Convenience in travel was paramount in his mind in 1974.

The Gideons were urgently requiring new premises for their headquarters, and after spending some hours one Sunday in August pondering and praying over the matter, he had come to the conclusion that for the good of the whole organisation a place within easy road and rail access of London and of the North and West was needed. The longer he thought and prayed, the deeper was the Rugby area impressed on his mind, so the following day he phoned the national president to tell him the result of his research. Then things moved quickly.

The national president got in touch with the vice-president, who reported the next day that his Manchester agent had heard of a very attractive office property in Lutterworth, within eight miles of Rugby, and only four miles from the M1 and M6 junction. On Thursday of that week they were looking it over, and on Friday, accompanied this time by the national treasurer, they went again and agreed unanimously that the Georgian house facing up a main road in the quiet market town, and within a stone's throw of John Wycliffe's memorial, was just what they wanted. It took a little longer to get through all the necessary legalities, but on October 1st the documents were signed, and in November Western House, George Street, Lutterworth, became the property of The Gideons International in the British Isles.

This was the third time they had moved since starting in John Street, London W1. Sharply rising rents had driven them, like many other organisations, from the capital, and for a time they had occupied part of a modern office block in Reading. But now the work was increasing rapidly, and when it got to the point of the boardroom also doing duty as stockroom, typist's office and collating room, it became evident that the seams were at the point of bursting. The body, so to speak, had outgrown the suit, and needed a new outfit. Hence the move to Lutterworth.

If it was in a more remote spot than formerly, with fewer visitors dropping in unannounced, the telephone rang more frequently than ever. Someone had to do duty as telephonist all day, and for months on end Rita Hall took on the job. It was not what she had been accustomed to as a missionary's wife in India, but she soon became adept at dealing with the unexpected. So when a young man's voice came over the wires one day, asking in an agitated manner, "Can you help me?" she answered calmly.

"I will if I can – how?"

Then followed a rather garbled story of how, as a schoolboy, he had dabbled with the Ouija board and the occult, until he had had a bad fright and given it all up. What was upsetting him now was that someone he'd known at that time had turned up unexpectedly, stayed the night, and was still there.

"And what worries me is that he's got those cards and things connected with the occult spread out on the floor. They scare me." He sounded alarmed, and came out with his request. "When I was at school I was given a Gideon New Testament and now I can't find it when I want it. I need it. So I'm phoning to ask if you can let me have another one?"

"Certainly," said Rita. "Give me your name and address." She was thinking quickly as she wrote it down. There was more to this than just a desire for the New Testament. The young man was frightened, aware of an evil which he could not define, and did not know how to combat. It was not enough just to send him the New

Testament he had asked for. She heard behind that polite but agitated voice a cry for help, and knew she could not ignore it.

"So you live in Sheffield?" she asked chattily. She did not know what to do, but realised she must keep him talking. After a few more casual remarks she said. "You know, I believe it would be a tremendous help to you if a Gideon in the neighbourhood came to see you."

"A Gideon here in Sheffield?" The young man was evidently surprised. "Do you have Gideons all over the place then? Do you mean that one could actually come here and see me?"

"Yes, I'm sure of it. He could bring you the New Testament, too. I'll phone our branch in Sheffield and see what they can do. Let me have your number and I'll ring you back after I've got in touch with them."

He gave his number, and Rita got through to the home of a Gideon in Sheffield. His wife answered the phone, and when Rita explained the situation to her she said immediately, "Of course! This very day. We'll go together."

Rita dialled the young man's number and when he answered said, "Someone will be coming round to see you as soon as possible. Just wait in – they'll come. Let me know how you get on. Goodbye," and rang off. There was no more to say to him – there was a lot more to say to God.

Next morning, amid the many phone calls she answered, one was always to stand out in her memory. Responding to the ringing bell she lifted the receiver and heard a confident young voice say, "May I speak to Mrs. Hall, please? I'm the fellow from Sheffield. Yes, they came. They took me back with them for the night. Helped me no end." Then he went on, "It's wonderful! I gave my heart to the Lord! Everything's all right. Thank you Mrs. Hall!"

Another call, a year or two later, was even more urgent. A man's voice, saying he was in a hotel in Bristol, continued wildly, "I can't stand any more. My marriage is breaking up. Everything's gone wrong in my life. I'm going to end it all right here in this room."

Rita stiffened. This was critical. She'd heard several of the Gideon reports of people who had been on the verge of suicide in a hotel room, but never had she been involved herself, and now here she was, alone in the office, with a would-be suicide at the other end of the line. If he rang off she'd have no idea who he was, how he could be stopped. At all costs, she must keep him talking.

"I'm glad you've got in touch," she said. "We're here to help you. What made you phone The Gideons?"

"There's a Bible in this bedroom. I saw the telephone number."

She asked him about his job, trying to get his mind on ordinary matters. "Working on an exhibition stall? Does that involve unusual working hours?" If only someone would come into the office who could take this call!

"Just what is it that's troubling you right now?" she asked gently. Death – death. That was all he wanted. It was the only way out.

She kept the conversation going for half an hour and then, to her relief, a door opened and Brian Hickford, the office manager, appeared. She couldn't have wished for anyone better at the moment. Always cheerful, able to adapt himself to any company, he could cope with any sort of situation. He was on his way to the stockroom, but a smiling glance in her direction brought him swiftly over to her desk in response to her urgent signal. She went on talking as calmly as ever, but her free hand was scribbling feverishly on the pad beside her, telling Brian what was happening.

"I'll take the call for you – put him through to the next office," he whispered, and disappeared through the door.

Then Rita heard a click, knew he had taken up the receiver, and said to the man in the Bristol hotel, "There's a Gideon here who'd like to speak to you," heard Brian's hearty voice greeting him, and thankfully rang off.

Then the other phone rang. It was the receptionist of the Bristol hotel.

"Have you been speaking to someone from this hotel?"

she asked. "He's been holding up the line for half an hour, and every time I try to speak to him he abuses me."

"The young man is in a very disturbed frame of mind," replied Rita. "He's threatening to commit suicide. One of my male colleagues is talking to him now."

"Oh!" The telephonist was alarmed. "Please keep him talking. I must get the manager," and rang off.

Then the Lutterworth police arrived. They had been called from Bristol, and found Brian still on the phone.

"Keep him talking," they whispered, and Brian continued, listening to the wild talk about death – reasoning, comforting, encouraging until, at the end of the longest two hours of his life, the conversation ended with the arrival of the police in the hotel bedroom in Bristol.

But that was not the end of the story. The man, having committed no criminal act, was taken by his wife, who came for him from London, into the psychiatric ward of a hospital for treatment. He had been under pressure at work and at home, felt he needed God but did not know how to find Him, tried transcendental meditation which made matters worse, then in the hotel bedroom found the Gideon Bible, opened it at John 3, and read, "Ye must be born again... Can he enter the second time into his mother's womb and be born?"

It was at this point, thoroughly confused and feeling desperate, that he had phoned The Gideons' office.

When Brian put down the receiver he did not finish with the case. He wrote to the man, visited him, put him in touch with a Gideon living near enough to see him regularly, and introduced him to an evangelical vicar. Some time later the man drove up to Lutterworth with his wife and family – not to see the Wycliffe memorial nor even The Gideons headquarters. He had come to visit Brian and tell him he had found God through faith in Christ, joined the Church, and had no more thoughts about death. Life was too well worth living!

*   *   *

One of the regulations of The Gideons International is that no member of the National Executive shall hold office for more than three consecutive years. This results in a constant change in leadership and freshness of emphasis as each newly-elected member brings the contribution of his own personality and experience.

When Henry M. Sibthorpe was elected as vice-president, then president, and after ten years national chaplain, no one who knew him had any doubt as to what he would emphasise. Personal evangelism was his line. The proprietor of the chain of stores in Cornwall that bore the name West End Department Stores Limited was even better known for his enthusiasm in telling people about Christ than for his acumen in business, though there was ample evidence for that, too. He and his brother had conducted beach missions for children for years, he was in constant demand to speak at meetings, and the commercial travellers who visited him knew that the goods they had come to sell would not provide the only topic of conversation.

"You ought to join The Gideons," said one of them to him one day, and went on to tell him something about the organisation. Henry Sibthorpe had never heard of it before, but he made up for lost time by enrolling as a member as soon as possible, found out all he could about it, and decided it was just what he had been needing to expand his activities and reinforce his affirmation that Christ was the only deliverer of man from all his sins and troubles. The Personal Worker Testament, which is produced for Gideons to use when talking to individuals, became part of his stock in trade. He always had one or two in the pocket of his car, ready to pass on to anyone who showed a genuine interest, while his Gideon badge provided a useful point at which to open the conversation.

"Ever seen one of these before?" he would ask. It really did not matter whether the answer was yes or no, since an explanation of what The Gideons were doing and why they were doing it followed either naturally enough, and was the means of directing the listener's thoughts into areas in the mind and conscience all too often kept firmly sealed off.

It happened that way one day when Sibthorpe, driving away from Heathrow Airport, picked up a young hitch-hiker who asked for a lift to Exeter. As they cruised along the leafy roads of Surrey and Hampshire, Henry Sibthorpe talked in his cheerful, friendly manner about the reality of Christ's presence in the life of the believer, every now and then interposing a question which demanded some sort of an answer. The young man was ill at ease at first, but gradually relaxed and, when he started talking, his reason for leaving Birmingham in a hurry came out. It was not a happy one. He had committed forgery, been found out, was now on the run, and wanted to get right away before the police could catch up with him.

Henry Sibthorpe drove silently on for a minute or two, then said quietly, "It's God you're really running away from, you know. If the law gets you all you can expect is justice. If you turn to God, it will be different. From Him you can expect mercy," and went on to tell him the reason for Christ's death. "Let's draw in here," he suggested as they approached a lay-by, and when the car came to a halt, reached his hand out for the New Testament. "I want to show you what the Word of God says. Read it for yourself.

"If we confess our sins, He is faithful and just to forgive us our sins, and to cleanse us from all unrighteousness."

They sat together for an hour in the car, talking, looking slowly and seriously in the New Testament, as Sibthorpe pointed to one and then another of the promises to those who repented. Then he said gently,

"These are God's words. Do you believe them? Do you want Christ to come into your life?" and when the young man nodded silently he just bowed his head and said, "Shall we both pray, then?" . . .

When the car pulled out of the lay-by and proceeded on the South-West road again, there was a different expression on the young man's face and a new determination in his manner.

"I don't know quite what I'm going to do," he said.

"But Christ will show me, won't He?"

"And give you strength to do what's right, and set your feet on a straight path," Sibthorpe said reassuringly. "Here's my card. Keep in touch. I'll be praying for you."

A few weeks later he heard from the young man. He'd gone back to Birmingham, owned up to his crime, taken his punishment but with peace in his heart, and was now going forward as a Christian.

This was only one of many such incidents in Henry Sibthorpe's colourful life, so he always had plenty of up-to-date stories with which to embellish his sermons. On one occasion, when the *Daily Mail* carried an illustrated news item about a Bible presentation in Dartmoor Prison, he was the main speaker, and some time later the prison chaplain forwarded a letter to him written by a Nigerian who was serving a long prison sentence. The letter ran:

> I am taking this opportunity to thank you for the message which struck to the root of my heart. When I opened the Bible which you presented to me, I began by exploring the fact of Christ perhaps merely intellectually and theologically. But now I know the fact that Christ is about to explore me spiritually and morally, me, a prodigal son who has spent eight years of my life in prison.
>
> I began by dealing with a historic figure as represented in the Gospel and gradually I became aware that the ultimate reality and heart of things is dealing with me in my lonely cell.

Sibthorpe read on. There was a depth about this man's writing that surprised him.

> I set about to see what I could find in Christ. I know now that God in Christ has found me.
>
> My one aim in life now is to serve Him with all my heart, mind, body and soul. I have heard you say to us that you are willing to help anyone who is willing to serve Him, and I am now appealing to you for such

help. Help me to see Him as you have seen Him. Help
me to serve Him as you are now serving Him. I will
devote the whole of my life to serve Him, mind, body
and soul among my own people, anywhere in Africa,
and to tell them that as my sins which are many are now
forgiven, even so may theirs be. And to help them to live
for Christ even as you will help me.

The reality of that young Nigerian's faith was tested
through a further two years in prison, during which time
he earned the title of "The Dartmoor Miracle." When
eventually he was released, he spent his first weekend of
freedom in the Sibthorpe's hospitable home. Then he took
the plane back to Nigeria, wrote to his Gideon friends
frequently, and after some months announced that he had
been made chief of his tribe in the place of his father, who
had died while he was in prison.

But that was not all, nor was it the most important news
he had to impart.

"You will be glad to know that I and my people have
established a church," he wrote, adding that already they
had doubled their numbers, and others were being added
daily. He had a quaint way of explaining the reason for
this. Sibthorpe's face crinkled in a little smile as he read,
"There is no doubt at all that our Lord has had a hand in
it."

He would not have put it in quite that way himself, but
he cordially agreed with the sentiment expressed. The
Lord had had a hand in it.

The Lord had had a hand in it in other places, too.
Burundi, for instance...

11   "Our Lord had a Hand in it"

The Gideon work in Burundi may be said to be the story of one little New Testament. It had been given to a missionary nurse in a distribution by members of The Auxiliary in the USA in 1953, and some eighteen years after receiving it, it was still in her possession. It was a handy size, and the references on the first few pages were the sort she found very useful when talking to patients about their problems. However, the little book got working in quite an unexpected way in 1971, when the missionary nurse sat looking at it pensively, conscious of a strangely persistent urge to do something which she felt to be quite beyond her.

On the face of it, the idea that had lodged itself in her mind was ridiculous. How could she possibly get a copy of a Gospel into the hands of every primary school student in Burundi? She knew that for most of those students, many of them adults, their academic education would begin and end in the primary school, and their scanty libraries consisted of little more than tattered textbooks and trashy novels. What it would mean if even a small part of God's Word could find its way into those pathetic collections! But to provide them all, approximately 120,000 copies would be required, and even if she had the money to buy them, which she hadn't, how could she set about the distribution?

However, the idea persisted, so she started to pray about it, and then The Gideons came to mind. After all, the very New Testament she was holding in her hand right now had been a gift from their organisation. They gave Bibles away – that was what they were known for. They might be willing to do something along that line for needy Burundi. So she decided to get in touch with them, and wrote to their international headquarters in the USA. Could they provide her with large numbers of Scriptures – if so, she'd find a way of distributing them somehow. . .

The response was encouraging. Certainly they would help. But they would do it in the Gideon way. It might take a little longer than the immediate distribution for which she hoped, but it would be more effective and lasting. They had their well-tried methods of procedure, and what they required from her at this stage was a list of pastors in Burundi who would be able to recommend to them Christian business and professional men in the country who might become Gideons. This was the Gideon method, they explained. They worked in conjunction with national Christians who were in the business world of their own country. Bible distribution would only start after a Gideon branch had been formed.

So a missionary nurse, a woman, found herself in the unusual role of laying the foundation of a branch of an organisation which is exclusively male. Undisturbed by this aspect of the case, if it occurred to her at all, she set about her task. She was in a good position to interview pastors of churches in Burundi, so taking her little New Testament with her as a sample of what would be provided if a Gideon branch were formed, she explained the idea to them, and obtained the lists which The Gideons International had requested.

Things went well for a time. Ten business men of Burundi became prospective Gideons, met regularly for prayer, and were only awaiting the arrival of a Gideons International headquarters representative to enrol them as members and establish a branch, when all their plans went to the winds. A bitter civil war broke out which lasted for months, and in the executions that took place nightly, six of the prospective Gideons lost their lives.

During those terrifying days five little words came repeatedly to the mind of the missionary nurse, words that she had read time and time again in the past without seeing any significance in them. Indeed, they were words she would not even have found in one of the modern versions of the Bible. It is to be surmised that the same message would have come to her in another form had she not adhered to the King James Authorised Version of the Bible, but as it was, that was the one with which she was most familiar, and it was there that they lit up for her in an entirely new, almost prophetic manner.

"And it came to pass," she read in Luke 2:1, and stopped short. In so casual a way was an event recorded which must have brought about an incredibly chaotic situation at the time. Augustus Caesar, world ruler of his day, had issued a decree which resulted in thousands of people taking to the road to go and register in their native towns. Among them were Joseph and Mary the mother of Jesus. Little wonder there was no room for them in the inn at Bethlehem. It was a time of upheaval, perhaps as disturbing as the upheaval in Burundi now. In the light of history that decree was merely an event that had happened. Once it was over things had settled down again, and the purpose of God through it all had been accomplished.

Just as the power of Augustus Caesar had apparently determined the birthplace of Jesus Christ, and eventually passed away, leaving the unassailable evidence that Bethlehem, as foretold centuries before, was the destined spot, so this apparently shattering upheaval would pass too, and the purpose of God remain.

And so it came to pass. At last peace was restored in Burundi. In the summer of 1974 the international field representative of The Gideons arrived, and on August 2nd, Burundi became the hundredth country in which a Gideon branch had been established. The Bible distribution could start in earnest – and because a Gideon branch had been established, it would continue.

Burundi was not the only country in which The Gideons saw that "our Lord had a hand in it," even in the political upheavals of the early 1970s. Perhaps the most spectacular evidence of this was in the distribution of Scriptures to the whole of the South Korean Army.

The opening of this extraordinarily wide door of opportunity came about in the first place through the astute observations of a general in the Army who was not a Christian, but a Buddhist. General Shin Han had lived before the outbreak of the Korean war in North Korea, and had noticed that the religion which seemed to provide the most effective bulwark against the encroachments of Communism was Christianity. He knew that what people believed affected their whole lives, and also motivated their loyalties, and what he wanted now, as general in command of the South Korean First Army, was the loyalty of his men. Since Christianity, with its basic belief that there is One True God, is diametrically opposed to Communism, with its basic belief that there is not, he saw in it a metaphysical reason for men to adhere to the one and oppose the other. And since Christians were men of integrity who were prepared to stand up for what they believed in the face of persecution and danger, he was convinced that more of them in the armed forces would be a strength to morale where it was most needed.

Generals in command of armies are not usually the dilly-dallying sort. Certainly General Shin Han was not. Having arrived at his conclusion regarding the best bulwark against Communism, he invited the chief of chaplains of the First Army to do everything possible to convert the entire South Korean Army to Christianity. And the sooner the better.

It was a tall order, but the chaplain was the man for the job. The general's motives might be political, but as far as he was concerned he saw in this official assignment the opportunity of the century to evangelise the armed forces of his own country. He grasped it without hestitation. He organised mass meetings to hear gifted preachers, instituted daily services in the barracks, and in addition to that, encouraged the men to study for themselves the Christian's holy book, the Bible. What Mao Tse Tung's "Little Red Book" was to the people of China, the New Testament should be to the armed forces of South Korea.

That is how The Gideons came on the scene. They were invited to supply the entire Army with New Testaments, and to do it in the Gideon way, making the presentations publicly and explaining what The Gideons were doing and why they were doing it.

There were no more than ten branches of The Gideons in the whole of South Korea, but they set about complying with the request they had received. Korean Gideons took time off from their work to visit military camps all over the country. Off they went with their Gideon displays and their Gideon banners, shaking hands cordially with commanding officers who stood in the presence of their assembled companies to accept on their behalf the stacks of New Testaments to be distributed among them. If there were newsmen with cameras to report the events, so much the better. The Korean Gideons, as business men, subscribed to the adage that it pays to advertise.

It was an inspiring time. The American Gideons, who supplied the New Testaments, followed the crusade with fervent interest. Then, as news of baptisms by the hundred reached them, accompanied by letters from pastors and chaplains expressing the conviction that the circulation of the New Testament was largely responsible for the turning to Christ of so many, they produced an illustrated booklet for distribution among Gideon members world-wide entitled *Korea* telling the whole story briefly, and concluding with a message from the chaplain-in-chief of the Republic of South Korea Army, in which he wrote.

"I am especially grateful to God for providing the Gideon ministry to supply the Word of God to the Korean servicemen... This has resulted in the salvation of thousands of Korean servicemen. Approximately 50,000 Korean servicemen were baptised during the last two years, and now there are 200,000 servicemen who are Christians in the Korean Army at the end of 1972..."

When the apostle Paul, writing to the believers in Corinth, made a point of telling them about the generosity of those in Macedonia in sending help to Christians in Judaea, he was doing more than a bit of reporting, and he admitted it. He had a reason for mentioning the matter. The Macedonian believers were providing him with just the sort of example he needed to hammer home his precept. He hoped to stimulate the Corinthians to similar action.

"Our desire is not that others might be relieved while you are hard pressed, but that there might be equality. At the present time, your plenty will supply what they need..." he wrote. "That there might be equality... your plenty will supply what they need."

The Gideons International may or may not have had the same idea in mind when they produced the booklet on Korea, but there is little doubt that the unspoken challenge it contained had its effect on other national associations. It was too clear an evidence of what could be attained when the "haves" at the base supplied what was needed to the "have nots" at the front for the message to be overlooked.

In the light of what the American Gideons were doing, the British Isles branch, by this time fully self-supporting, could not rest content. For years it had been at the receiving end of finance poured in from the The Gideons International resources. Now was the time to reverse the order, and start being at the giving end instead. There were Gideon branches in well over a hundred countries now, and that sounded fine when statistics were rattled off, but when the true situation of them all was revealed, the picture was not so rosy. Some were in the "Third World", oppressed by political strife and economic hardship. Without support from Gideons in the wealthier nations of the West, they could scarcely hope to survive, let alone extend their activities.

The booklet on Korea, with its inspiring evidence of what had been accomplished because The Gideons on the spot had been fully supported by The Gideons in America and Canada, provided a powerful incentive for Gideons in the British Isles to follow their example. The membership was encouraged to start giving sacrificially to the International Extension Fund even though development work in the British Isles had still not been completed. The funds started to flow. Then, as the decade rolled on, there was a further development organised by the International

Extension Committee. Not only should Bibles be sent, but distributors also, men who would travel at their own charges to help their fellow Gideons in a "Bible blitz".

This was something new. Gideons had travelled from the ends of the earth to attend International conventions, listening to reports from various countries, shaking hands with men who wore the same badge but whose language they could not speak, eating at the same table and laughing cheerfully at the variety of ways in which English can be misunderstood. They had sat side by side at meetings where talks were interpreted, murmured a fervent "Amen" to prayers they had scarcely understood. What most Gideons had not done before was to stand by the roadside in a foreign land handing out New Testaments to crowds of vociferous young students emerging from school; to bump along for hours over pot-holed tracks on visits to hotels and hospitals in remote areas; and to get glimpses of life below the surface of the type that Vernon Whitby-Smith, of Staffordshire, reported after he arrived home again: "Our visit to Kumasi Gaol was an experience never to be forgotten. One thousand men aged between eighteen and eighty were just herded before us, ill clad, some covered in sores from head to toe, some with missing limbs, some blind, some having been there for forty years." The Gideon team consisted of two Ghanaians and two westerners, and after they had explained the way of eternal life through faith in Christ Jesus, the New Testaments were distributed. "Seeing the way the men looked at us, as one by one they threaded themselves through the opening in the gate, leaves indelible memories..."

The Gideon from Staffordshire had another memory, too – the bewildered, empty expression in the eyes of a couple of raggedly-dressed eleven-year-old boys locked away behind a black iron door where they were being imprisoned for stealing.

"After talking to the policemen, who work under appalling conditions, we pleaded with the chief inspector to release these two boys, which he did," Vernon continued, adding slowly, "but the memory of those four eyes will, I'm sure, live in my mind for all time."

Other Gideons from the British Isles joined international teams about that time, going to Nigeria, Singapore, Hong Kong and India. The Ulster representative from the British Isles, George Smith, was so distressed by the poverty and destitution he saw on the streets on the way from the airport when he arrived in India, that he knew he would not sleep, even if he went to bed. The indefinable sense of evil that lay behind some of those scenes was too oppressive.

"Oh, God, why did you ever send me here?" he cried up in his hotel room. It was hard even to pray. And God, who knows how to comfort those who are cast down, comforted him in a simple, warm, human way. Unable to settle to anything, the unhappy man decided he'd go down to the coffee shop for a strong cup of coffee. As he was drinking it two strangers came in. He glanced at them idly, then his eyes dropped down to the lapels of their coats, and he jumped eagerly to his feet. They were wearing Gideon badges. ("Always wear your badge!" he exclaimed as he related the incident later.) Nothing could have cheered him more. All depression was dispelled as they talked together for hours, non-stop, these men who had come to India, not for pleasure or sightseeing, but to do business for God. They were knit together immediately, and his heart soared as they were joined by others – Gideons from Sweden, Norway, Australia, Canada and the USA who had come to do a job of work together. They were hard at it for eight days, starting with a prayer meeting at 5.30 a.m. followed by breakfast.

"We were then organised into groups of three or four with one Indian Gideon, and went off to our first presentation . . . Each day we worked right through till the schools closed, then concentrated on hotels." The period was peppered with memorable experiences. Standing together in a little group, arms round each other as they prayed for wisdom in seeking an entrance into a Bombay school that had hitherto refused The Gideons, and coming away some time later having seen the principal and handed out some 800 Testaments. Offering a Testament to a friendly café owner who, as he saw it, gasped, "God has sent you to me! I've been searching for an English Bible!" – with the eventual result that an opening was made for local Christians to preach in his community. Explaining to an inquisitive waiter in Hyderabad what the team of western men staying in the hotel had been doing, and eliciting from him an admission that he had been putting off committing his life to Christ, but that he now intended to delay no longer. Over and above all that was the impression made upon George Smith by the dedication of the Indian Gideons. "Their Christian character and their singular desire that their fellow countrymen might know Christ as Saviour has, I am glad to confess, left such an impression that I could never be, nor want to be, the same again."

The International Extension Scheme was having a twofold effect. It would be difficult to decide whether Gideons who went to Third-World countries, or the Third-World countries to which they went, derived the greater benefit. On the basis of the ninth Beatitude[1] however, it is perhaps safe to assume that the Gideons who gave were the happier.

* * *

The year 1982 will long be remembered in the British Isles as the year of the Falklands crisis. It came as a shock to the whole nation to learn that Argentinian forces had landed on the islands and then, a short time later, that a British task force was being prepared to go and turn them off again. It was headline news for weeks, with newspapers, television and radio broadcasting each move or anticipated move of the politicians, and following closely the progress of the ships that were sailing the 8,000 miles down to the South Atlantic.

The whole thing had evidently caught the Prime

[1] "It is more blessed to give than to receive."

Minister, the Foreign Secretary, and nearly everyone else by surprise, and the fact that HMS *Invincible* had been furnished with Bibles and Testaments before she sailed was in no way due to The Gideons having prophetic knowledge of what would happen. It was simply that the branch in Furness, alert to what was going on in the local shipyard, had noticed that the newest and largest ship in the Royal Navy was nearing completion, and had written to the commanding officer offering to supply the ship with New Testaments. The offer was accepted. Four Gideons and their wives went aboard on Navy Sunday, 1980, and the presentation of a hundred Testaments was duly made to the chaplain. From the point of view of the Furness and Portsmouth Gideons, it was only part of their regular programme of distribution.

The same applied to the North Liverpool branch. Over the years they had supplied Gideon Scriptures to at least twenty naval ships, including HMS *Sheffield*. The manner in which it was done was dependent on the ship's captain or the chaplain. In some cases Testaments were given to every member of the crew. In other cases the chaplain asked for a supply to be distributed at his own discretion. The arrangement suited everyone, and if The Gideons were not always able to place as many Testaments in each ship as they had hoped, they were glad of the opening. It could be followed up with replacements later, as required.

Replacements were not required to the extent that The Gideons hoped. When things were peaceful, and life was pursuing its accustomed course, there was little interest in the small blue Testaments to be found in the lockers or obtained from the chaplain. It was not until the ships were steaming on, week after week, into unknown seas, far from any friendly shore, that the young servicemen who had set off, bound for the Falklands on a wave of patriotic ardour, started to feel uneasy. Crammed together with nothing to do they began facing the prospect of going into battle – not the mock conflicts in which their skills and alertness and endurance had been tested, but the real thing.

They had thought, when they joined up, that they had life before them. It was dawning on them now that possibly what lay ahead was not life, but death. Then it was that the demand for Bibles began to be acute and the need for replacements was realised in mid-ocean where they could not be obtained. One young serviceman who had a Gideon New Testament wrote saying he dared not lay it down even for a second in case it should be "nicked", and that he could have sold it a hundred times over for any price he asked. Urgent requests were sent home, various organisations as well as The Gideons rushed into action, hurrying to supply Bibles by any means possible – but it was the quiet stockpiling of the years of peace that met the sudden, immediate craving for the Word of God.

"I feel as if I have been placed right in the middle of a huge mission field almost totally unprepared," wrote an RAF officer on the cross-channel ferry, *St. Edmund,* that – like many other passenger ships – had been pressed into service with the task force. "Many are seeking God for the first time. Praise the Lord that this ship is full to the gunwales with NIV Bibles placed by The Gideons! What an opportunity!" The Bibles were right there when they were most needed, as on a number of other ships such as the *QE II* and the *Canberra* – placed, in some cases, years before. It is better to prepare ahead of time for a possible emergency. When it happens, there is no time to prepare.

Young Lieutenant Clive Dytor was one of the Royal Marine Commandos of the Zulu Company who embarked on a ship bound for the Falklands in which there were Gideon New Testaments. His life had been pretty successful outwardly, but his conscience told him that if everything were revealed he wouldn't look so good. As the days passed, and the ship on which he was sailing steamed inexorably southwards into the unknown, he began to think. He looked at the little New Testament in his possession, opened it reflectively, and began to read, went on reading and began to pray. The weeks passed – five of them, with nothing but the ocean around and the sky overhead, the lull before the storm. It was during that lull that he made his decision.

"Today I want to start a new life," he wrote in a letter to Gideon headquarters in Lutterworth, thanking them for the enlightenment and hope their New Testament had given him. "I know it doesn't happen in a flash, but today I want to remember as the day that I dedicated my life to Christ. I believe! I believe! What a thrill it is to say that!" The storm broke for him not long afterwards, when he had to lead his men into battle, from which he emerged unharmed. In another letter of gratitude written to The Gideons he said, "Should you ever want to use my testimony of knowing God under fire, which I did, I'll be glad to help."

As it happened, he gained the Military Cross, and admitted to a friend that as a boy he had always wanted to be a success, but that now, although he was quite pleased, it didn't seem to matter all that much. He still wanted to be a success – but in another realm, and to gain a better reward.

12   While Day Lasts

The little square at the end of George Street in Lutterworth was very quiet that August day in 1983. In The Gideon headquarters morning prayers were over, and the staff members were dispersing to their various offices. Ian Hall felt a glow of satisfaction as he glanced at them filing out. It was a good team. He noticed Brian Hickford and Chris Byrne chuckling together as they walked away, and guessed what they were so cheerful about. An unexpected cheque had put the accounts in a very healthy condition. "The Lord's done it again!" he heard Brian say triumphantly as they disappeared.

They had both left better-paid jobs to become Gideon staff members, both expressed themselves thankful to be out of the rat race of the twentieth-century financial world, and Chris, who had joined more recently, was still slightly amazed when he stopped to think about it, at the way his personal affairs, which might have been badly disrupted by the change, had quietly slipped into gear.

As Ian stood back to let the typists pass by, he felt a tap on the shoulder, and heard Ronald Slee say, "Can you spare a few minutes, Ian? We ought to go over the autumn programme again. There are several more requests to visit branches – a couple of them planning New Members dinners..."

Ronald Slee had joined the team as promotion manager a few years before, switching in middle life from an established career in his native Cornwall to do so. His job in The Gideons included keeping in touch with the branches throughout the British Isles, coordinating development, organising New Member Plan dinners – and doing a good deal of it himself.

When they had finished their discussion, Ian ran briskly

up the stairs into his own office overlooking the square and sat down at his desk, filing cabinets at an angle beside him. On the wall to his right were the large reproductions of Wycliffe preaching by the village cross, and the Wycliffe Bible being read in church . . .

He liked those pictures. They gave him a sense of history, of the continuity of the work he was engaged in. And of its vitalising character. He had a profound confidence in the Bible as being the Word of the Living God, and of its efficacy to cleanse and heal, inspire and direct those who studied its pages with an unprejudiced mind.

The past nineteen years in The Gideons had provided all the proof of that he might have needed. When anyone asked a question about results from their distribution, his memory was flooded with experiences he himself had had, and those he had heard about from others.

Many of them were simple and undramatic, like that of the twelve-year-old schoolboy in Sittingbourne who received a New Testament at a school distribution on the understanding that, like John Nicholson, he would read it every day. Unlike most of his fellow-students he took his promise seriously, and started by reading a few verses each morning before breakfast. His parents never went to church and, as the only time he was taken there was on infrequent visits to his grandparents, he knew very little about the devotional life. All the same, after a while he felt it might be a good thing to pray as well as to read, so he knelt by his bed and prayed – simple, uninstructed little prayers, mainly about family matters. In his mid-teens he made a study of comparative religions, but soon decided that he'd been right in believing what he had read in the New Testament, and was going to stick to it.

Things went smoothly for the boy. He became head prefect of his school, and it was not until he was leaving that his headmaster said to him, "When you get to university, you may feel lonely – get in touch with the Christian Union there. You'll find friendly people that way." He had never before heard of a Christian Union, but on his arrival he asked to be put in touch with it, and for the first time in his life he found himself among a group of young people who believed, just as he did, about Jesus Christ. It was a revelation to him, seemed to light up something inside, open a fresh spring of joy in an already happy life. When he and a girl in the Christian Union fell in love with each other, life was complete.

The story was too good to be typical, but it was true, all the same, though The Gideons would probably never even have heard of it had it not been for Ian Coffey. Ian Coffey was an evangelist with the Movement for World Evangelisation and met that young man when visiting the university. Coffey's own story was a Gideon story, too, but of a different character, for as a teenager he was a rebel, and intended to remain one. He took advantage of a church house-party to have a cheap holiday, but had no intention at all of entering into any spiritual activities, and deliberately took no Bible with him. On Saturday evening the scheduled meeting commenced without any sign of young Coffey and his like-minded companion. They had taken themselves off to the convivial atmosphere of a local pub. As they sat drinking, Coffey's friend said: "Those people at the house-party are really enjoying themselves – our only enjoyment comes from a bottle." It was on their return, feeling not quite so cheerful as they pretended to be, that Coffey had a sudden strange urge, quite out of character, to read the very book he had deliberately left at home. Where could he lay hands on a Bible without drawing attention to himself?

Many times in later years he recounted how, at that moment of deeply-felt need, he opened the locker by his bed and saw one. It was almost as though it had been waiting for him. It shook him, and he took it out with hands that trembled slightly. Then he opened it at random, and his eyes fell on the familiar parable of the talents.

Again, it will be like a man going on a journey, who called his servants and entrusted his property to them. To one he gave five talents of money, to another two talents, and to another one talent, each according to his ability. Then he went on his journey . . .

After a long time the master of those servants returned and settled accounts with them . . .

The reading of that parable clinched matters for young Coffey. This thing was really going to happen. Sooner or later he'd have to give an account to God for all the benefits he had received, including that of a Christian home, and there would be no escaping it. He'd better get right with God right now! That very night, on his knees, he asked for forgiveness – and received it.

The finding of that Bible just at the time when he needed it, not only alerted him to the existence of The Gideons, but predisposed him permanently in favour of them. After he became an evangelist, he told Ian Hall, "Without exception, I have always found that where The Gideons have been they have left the door open for the Gospel, especially in schools. There have been countless occasions when the headmaster has opened the door for me, and other evangelists as well, to go into a school simply on the recommendation of a local Gideon. I have often been able to use a Gideon contact to persuade a headmaster that I am not a religious fanatic, for they are always men of good standing in the local community. Headmasters may not all like what they do, but they certainly seem to admire them for doing it."

From Coffey's observation and experience, the majority of the New Testaments distributed by The Gideons to secondary-school children went into homes in which there was no other copy of Holy Scripture, and as Ian Hall knew, some of those New Testaments were read, rather surreptitiously, by parents – like the Cornish mother who wrote to headquarters asking for a New Testament "like the one given to my son, who has now gone to university and taken it with him, as I have found so much help through reading it". A visit by Henry Sibthorpe to give it to her in person resulted in her coming to personal faith in Christ.

Very often the New Testament that had been accepted

casually and put away carelessly suddenly came into its own – as when a depressed young "hippie" who was starting on drugs, shocked at the death by mugging of an elderly woman in Wolverhampton, found himself asking seriously a question he had often heard others ask idly, "What is the world coming to? So much violence, so much heartlessness, what was it all about?" It was then that he remembered his Gideon New Testament. He found it at the back of a cupboard, and flicking the pages was arrested by the words "the last days". The last days? This had something to do with the future, a subject that had always interested him, so he started reading: "But mark this. There will be terrible times in the last days. People will be lovers of themselves, lovers of money, boastful, proud, abusive, disobedient to their parents, ungrateful, unholy, without love, unforgiving, slanderous, without self-control, brutal, not lovers of the good, treacherous, rash, conceited, lovers of pleasure..."

The words came with the force of a personal accusation levelled at him in a court of law. They described him so accurately that he was startled. He turned back the pages, and started reading in the Gospels, where the generous heart of Christ towards sinners was revealed, and as he did so he became conscious of a Presence in the room. It was so real that when, on reopening his eyes, he saw no one he was almost disappointed. But he knew who was there with him. "Jesus Christ," he prayed, not really knowing what to say. "Let me come to You..." And that is where the new life started for him.

Even simpler, less spectacular stories came in letters from schoolchildren.

"I received my New Testament during the first year at senior school... I am almost certain that I would have rejected Christ had it not been for the inspiration and hope so clearly headed and compactly written in your edition... A friend of mine, Rosa, who comes from Yugoslavia, was very interested to learn that I read the daily readings before I went to sleep each night, and I am hoping that you might send me a New Testament for her."

And another: "Eight years ago on December 8th, 1970, when I was a schoolboy of eleven years old, I was given a Bible by your society . . . I think that if I had not received this New Testament from The Gideons I would not have discovered Jesus as my Saviour, and for your generosity I would like to thank you greatly . . ."

Sometimes the stories were very moving, like that of the thirteen-year-old boy suffering from leukemia, who took his Gideon New Testament with him into hospital. "Look at this!" he said excitedly to his parents, pointing to a section he had found in Romans 8 under the sub-heading "Future Glory". So far from fearing death he was looking forward to it, and when he died so great an impression was made that a mother who knew her own son had cancer sent a special request for the book on "Future Glory."

As about 85 per cent of Gideon Bibles and New Testaments were presented in schools, it was always encouraging to hear what happened to some of them, though Ian was not unduly influenced in his assessment of the effectiveness of the distribution by apparent results. That, on aggregate, a larger percentage was evident from prisons than from schools could be accounted for by the fact that prisoners have more time on their hands, and are more likely to be conscious of a change within themselves than teenagers.

Basically, the opportunities presented by the distribution in hotels still made the strongest appeal to him. Each Bible could reach the largest number of people, many of them those that could not be reached by any other means. He thought of the millions of people who visited the British Isles every year, putting up in hotels sometimes merely overnight – like the man who stayed in the Skyline Hotel at Heathrow, turned to the Bible he found there, and followed some of the suggested readings in the introduction until he came to 1 Peter 1, and read: "For you have been born again, not of perishable seed, but of imperishable, through the living and enduring Word of God. For, all men are like grass, and all their glory is like the flowers of the field; the grass withers and the flowers fall, but the Word of the Lord stands for ever. And this is the Word that was preached to you.''

What happened then, in the solitude of that hotel room, was left as a memorial by the verses which had been underlined, inscribed in red ink in the margin, ''When I came to these words I fell on my face before God . . . Peter Smith, Stafford.''

The international president of The Gideons happened to be staying in the same hotel and in the same room a year or two later and came across it. Back in Michigan, USA, he related the incident to a group of pastors, one of whom came to him and said, ''That story you told us, it's quite true. Peter Smith is a member of my church now.''

Topping up Bibles in hotels where presentations have been made is a regular assignment in the Gideon branches. Very rarely are no replacements required. ''I think people must read them in the bath,'' one Gideon said. ''So often are pages stuck together, as though they've been wet.'' And quite often Bibles are just missing. One of them found its way to Rumania in the baggage of a Rumanian soldier who had come to London for a few days as secretary to his commanding officer. He had been taught that God is a myth, but reading that Bible convinced him otherwise. He was thrilled to discover that God was real and speaking to him through these pages. He told an English visitor on a camp site near Bucharest about it. ''After a few weeks I had read the New Testament right through and I gave my heart to the Lord . . . I was deeply troubled about stealing the Bible and prayed that God would open the way for me to talk to some English Christian who I hope will be able to get in touch with The Gideons to tell them I am sorry for taking away the Bible, but I pray that they will forgive me . . . Tell them that if a Bible had not been in that bedroom I would not have discovered Jesus as my Saviour.''

May many more Bibles go in that way, was The Gideons' reaction! How often did the same sort of thing happen of which they never heard, Ian wondered. How thankful he was for the outcome of the presentation made to Sir Charles Forte, commemorating the ten-millionth Bible distributed by The Gideons in the British Isles. In his response, Sir Charles had assured The Gideons that he would support their placing of Bibles in all the Trust House Forte hotels bearing his name. As he represented one of the biggest hotel and catering combines in the world, with hundreds of hotels in various countries, that promise was "quite a thing."

But Ian realised that he'd have to keep alert to such opportunities. A change of directorship in the great hotel and catering groups such as the Hilton and the Holiday Inns could result in a change of policy, by which the open door for Bible placements could be closed overnight. The same need for vigilance applied everywhere, and the challenge to be doing what could be done, where it could be done, while it could be done. He remembered the words of Jesus that sounded a warning to those who might be inclined to take their service too easily, "As long as it is day, we must do the work of him who sent me. Night is coming when no one can work."

He was in a reflective mood today, but the pile of letters on his desk reminded him that his allotted task was right at hand. There were arrangements to be made for visits of British Gideons to join the Extension teams abroad. One Gideon was already preparing to go to Indonesia in a few weeks' time, four more to Kenya in 1984. This outreach was closest to Ian's heart, for he had lived in a Third-World country too long ever to forget the need there. The Gideons Bible distribution had reached almost saturation point in the land of plenty in which he lived now. It was time not to stop but to share. The aim to provide a Bible for a Third-World country for every one distributed in the British Isles, and to provide fellow workers to encourage the new and often struggling Gideon branches in those countries, was foremost in his mind as he prepared for the day's work.

There were the usual number of letters to be answered from a variety of people – a schoolboy, a divorcee, a man who had seen a Bible in his hotel bedroom, the anxious father of a girl who had walked out of home and refused to return... He must deal with these first, choose suitable books or pamphlets to send them, find out if they would welcome a personal talk with a Gideon in their neighbourhood. He had been dictating for about half an hour when the telephone rang, and lifting the receiver he said, "Yes, this is the Gideon headquarters. Yes, of course we'll be glad to do what we can to help you. Where are you phoning from?..." He glanced across at his secretary as he spoke, and with a shake of the head indicated that he would probably be engaged for some time. No more dictation at present. "Yes, I've got plenty of time to listen. There's no need to hurry..."

His secretary had gathered her papers together, and was slipping across the room and out of the door, with an amused little smile on her face. She had remembered something her former employer had said when she gave notice, and told him where she would be working.

"I don't envy your new boss his job," he had said. "I've never yet met anyone who's read a Gideon Bible." He doubted whether anyone ever did.

She placed the sheaf of letters from people who *had* read Gideon Bibles on the desk beside her and took the cover off her typewriter.

How wrong he was!